Film Actresses

Volume 18

Jeanette MacDonald

Documentary study

Part 1

ISBN-13 : 978-1502957108
ISBN-10 : 1502957108

Dtp
and
graphic design

Iacob Adrian

Author statement

The actors and actresses are the the bricks .

The cast and crew are the plaster .

They stand on the foundation created by
producers and writers and directors .

All these people creates the great palace
of the art of film .

Iacob Adrian - 2013

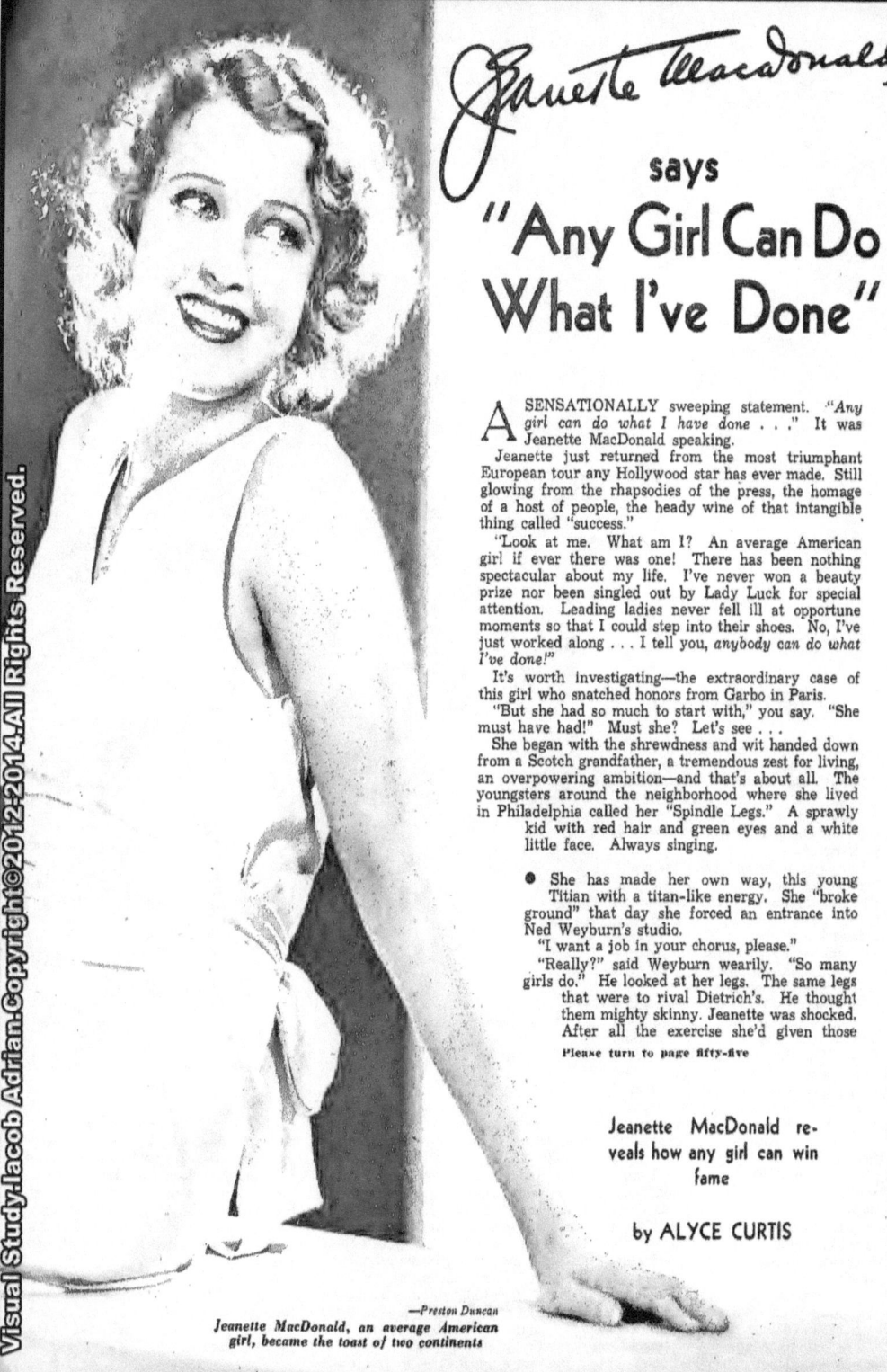

Jeanette Macdonald

says

"Any Girl Can Do What I've Done"

A SENSATIONALLY sweeping statement. *"Any girl can do what I have done . . ."* It was Jeanette MacDonald speaking.

Jeanette just returned from the most triumphant European tour any Hollywood star has ever made. Still glowing from the rhapsodies of the press, the homage of a host of people, the heady wine of that intangible thing called "success."

"Look at me. What am I? An average American girl if ever there was one! There has been nothing spectacular about my life. I've never won a beauty prize nor been singled out by Lady Luck for special attention. Leading ladies never fell ill at opportune moments so that I could step into their shoes. No, I've just worked along . . . I tell you, *anybody can do what I've done!*"

It's worth investigating—the extraordinary case of this girl who snatched honors from Garbo in Paris.

"But she had so much to start with," you say. "She must have had!" Must she? Let's see . . .

She began with the shrewdness and wit handed down from a Scotch grandfather, a tremendous zest for living, an overpowering ambition—and that's about all. The youngsters around the neighborhood where she lived in Philadelphia called her "Spindle Legs." A sprawly kid with red hair and green eyes and a white little face. Always singing.

● She has made her own way, this young Titian with a titan-like energy. She "broke ground" that day she forced an entrance into Ned Weyburn's studio.

"I want a job in your chorus, please."

"Really?" said Weyburn wearily. "So many girls do." He looked at her legs. The same legs that were to rival Dietrich's. He thought them mighty skinny. Jeanette was shocked. After all the exercise she'd given those

Please turn to page fifty-five

Jeanette MacDonald reveals how any girl can win fame

by ALYCE CURTIS

—Preston Duncan
Jeanette MacDonald, an average American girl, became the toast of two continents

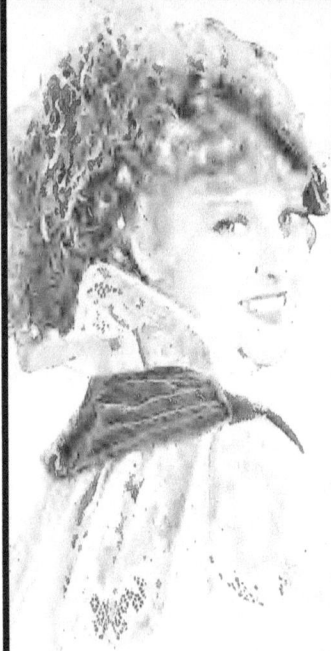

Jeanette MacDonald was never more charming than in The Merry Widow

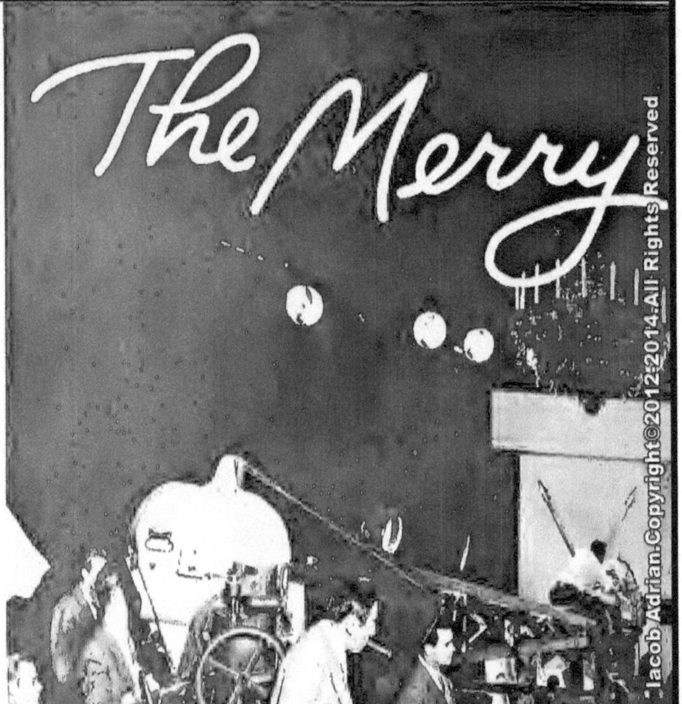

The Merry

by JACK SMALLEY

IT MUST BE catching, this virus of love. Maybe Cupid uses a special germ instead of arrows, for he most certainly infected *The Merry Widow* with romance.

Love was in the air during the making of this gorgeous Lehar operetta, Hollywood's most colorful production of the year, musically speaking, and I don't know whether it was brought onto the set by that mischievous fellow Lubitsch, or whether to just blame it on the waltz.

At all events, sheer happiness and a love thy neighbor spirit made bouyant and joyous the entire production. Never has Ernst Lubitsch been in gayer mood. That romantic contagion of his spread to everyone in the cast.

First off, he announced that he was going to hold a grand and glorious wedding for Jeanette MacDonald and her fiancé, Robert Ritchie!

"When we finish the picture, I open my house," he proclaimed, his black eyes sparkling. He waved his cigar at astounded Jeanette. "You think it is not big enough? To prove it, I invite everybody in Hollywood to your wedding!"

Jeanette nearly swooned. In vain she pointed out that Mr. Ritchie had just returned from Europe; they had no definite marriage plans; but Lubitsch would not listen. What could

be more delightful to celebrate the completion of his new home than a wedding? "I arrange everything," he tut-tutted. "Leave it all to me."

Just close your eyes a moment and visualize dynamic little Lubitsch. Wouldn't he make a dandy cupid, with that cigar cocked at an impish angle?

"But I am not ready for marriage," Jeanette told me earnestly. "When I marry, I wish to be able to settle down and make a career of it, and pictures are keeping me too busy to put on a domestic apron just now."

But she's in love — if you don't

believe it, go see *The Merry Widow*, Jeanette never looked more lovely. Even so, the camera can never give you the full flavor of her exquisite beauty, the copperish tint of her blonde hair, the flawless complexion, the—did I say cupid's virus was catching? But you'd fall in love with her too.

And then there's something brighter about the Chevalier smile in this production, and it isn't all due to the comedy of the plot or the lilt of Franz Lehar's waltzes.

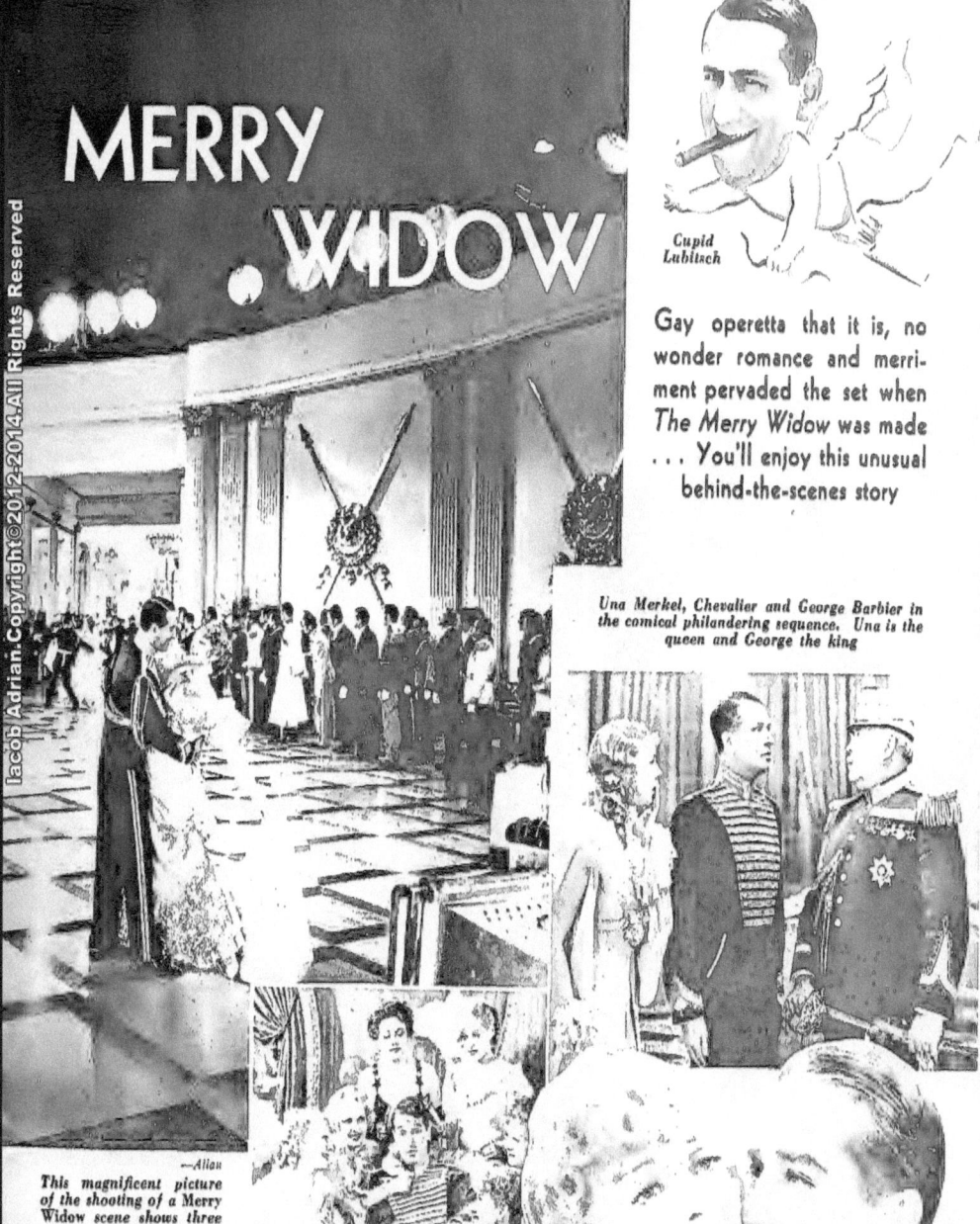

MERRY WIDOW

Cupid
Lubitsch

Gay operetta that it is, no wonder romance and merriment pervaded the set when *The Merry Widow* was made ... You'll enjoy this unusual behind-the-scenes story

Una Merkel, Chevalier and George Barbier in the comical philandering sequence. Una is the queen and George the king

—Allan

This magnificent picture of the shooting of a Merry Widow scene shows three cameras trained on the players while Director Lubitsch (with cigar) watches Jeanette MacDonald and Maurice Chevalier weave through the evolutions of Franz Lehar's romantic waltz

Just surrounded by loveliness, but the great Maurice seems to be a bit distraught in this scene

What a couple—Jeanette MacDonald and Chevalier in one of the picture's many romantic interludes

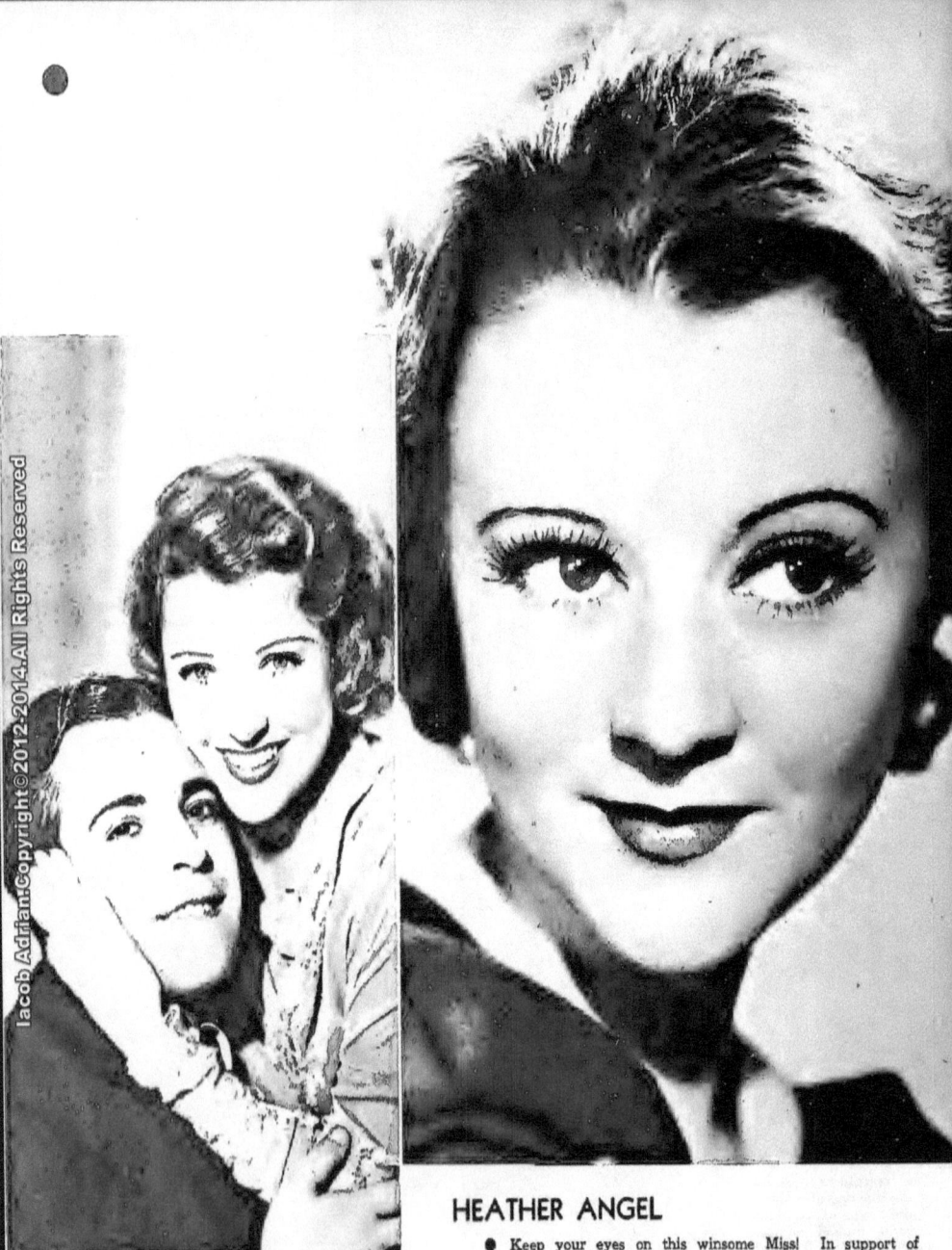

—Clarence Sinclair Bull

RAMON NOVARRO and JEANETTE MacDONALD

● Romance? Love? Wait until you see Ramón and Jeanette go into action in *The Cat and the Fiddle*, the picturization of the popular musical play!

HEATHER ANGEL

● Keep your eyes on this winsome Miss! In support of Leslie Howard in *Berkeley Square* she displays her great histrionic genius. Another of her new films is *Seven Lives Were Changed*

The Merry, Merry Widow

The picture was hardly underway when he caught it too. After seeing Kay Francis for years, suddenly the Chevalier eyes opened, and those who watched nodded sagely and said: "It's love!"

Oh, they all deny it. That's what adds zest to Hollywood romances; you're just good pals, always. Take out a marriage license and you're just being good pals. Get a divorce—still pals.

"Loff? Oh-h-h-h no!" grins Chevalier. "You should give me a chance to enjoy life before you take me to the altar again, no? I was such a long time married! As soon as I finish this picture, pouf, I am off. I go to Cannes for three months, then maybe a picture in England."

Meanwhile he and Kay Francis are seen everywhere together, raven tresses close to the boyish haircut of Maurice.

And Lubitsch was having the time of his life playing cupid, cut-up, and comedian, with a bit of directing thrown in sort of incidently. He was always up to some new mischief.

He had the time of his life "ribbing" the pretty girls in the lavish scene picturing the interior of Maxim's. These girls were to gather at the door and welcome Chevalier, ending up by lifting him above their heads while he laughs: "Oh, girls, it's great to be in loff!" Lubitsch had them lifting Chevalier until their arms ached. Did they get back at him? Wait.

Then he aimed a "rib" at Marcel Achard, famed French author who handles the dialog in the French version of the picture. The two versions are made simultaneously; the English cast steps aside and the French cast steps in for each "take," with Chevalier and Miss MacDonald changing from English to French for the two versions.

A great dane, Prince, plays an important part in the picture, and it was necessary to register the dog's bark. This was shot. Then Lubitsch called back the dog and his trainer.

"Now we have the dog bark with a French accent," he announced, glancing sideways at Achard. The Frenchman swallowed hard. He said he did not understand.

"For the French version, I insist the dog bark in French," Lubitsch said. Then he could no longer keep a straight face. And for that, the director was fated to be repaid.

Next he singled out Bela Loblov, who was imported to play a solo on that priceless violin of his. The Gypsy violinist was summoned for the take. Lubitsch went to elaborate lengths to get silence. He made an announcement; this was to be the highlight of the picture, nothing must prevent Bela from recording the solo perfectly. Cameras started; unforgettable music poured from the violin.

"Now we play it back," Lubitsch said. The order for a play-back flashed to the sound room. In a moment the recording

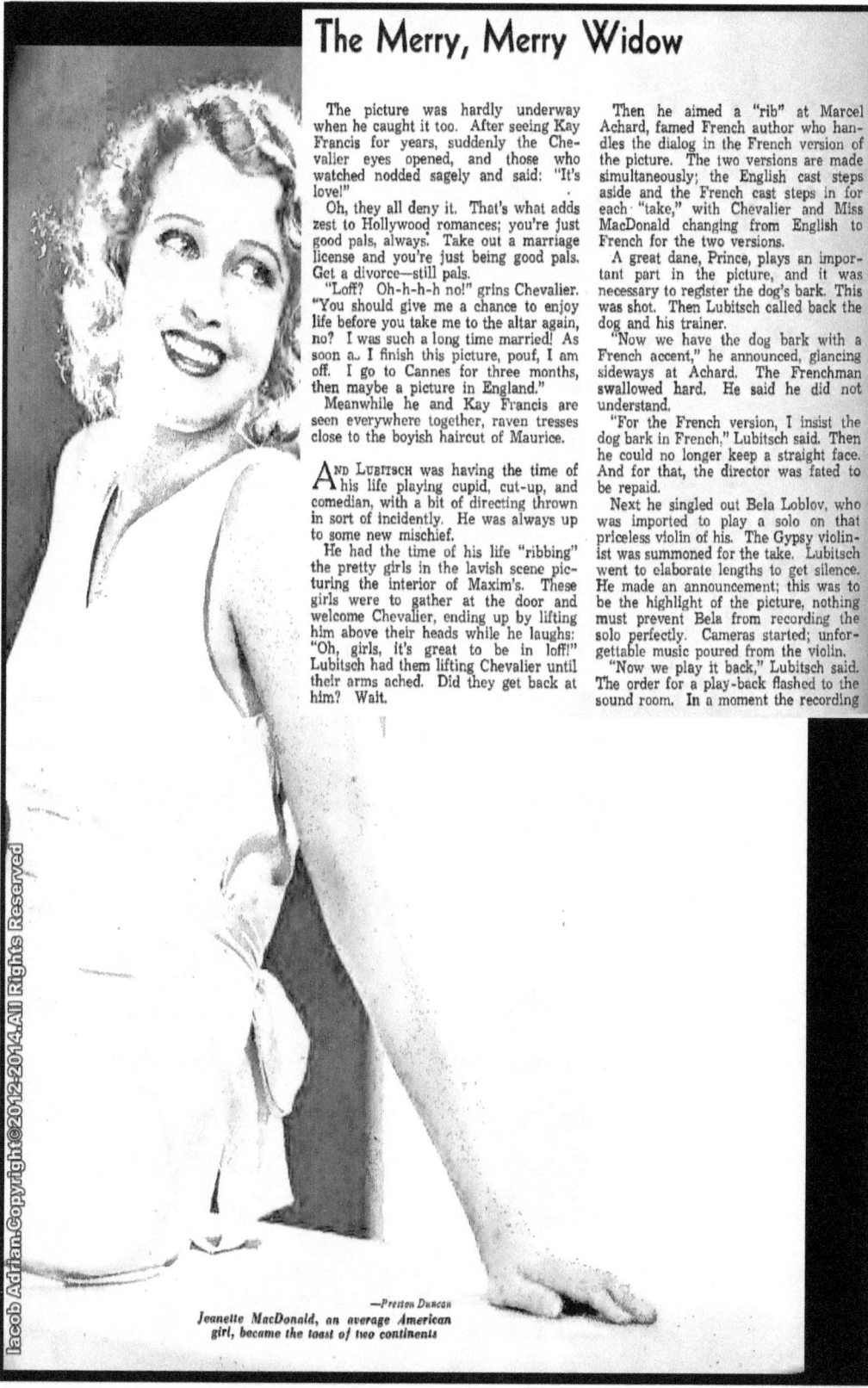

—Preston Duncan
Jeanette MacDonald, an average American girl, became the toast of two continents

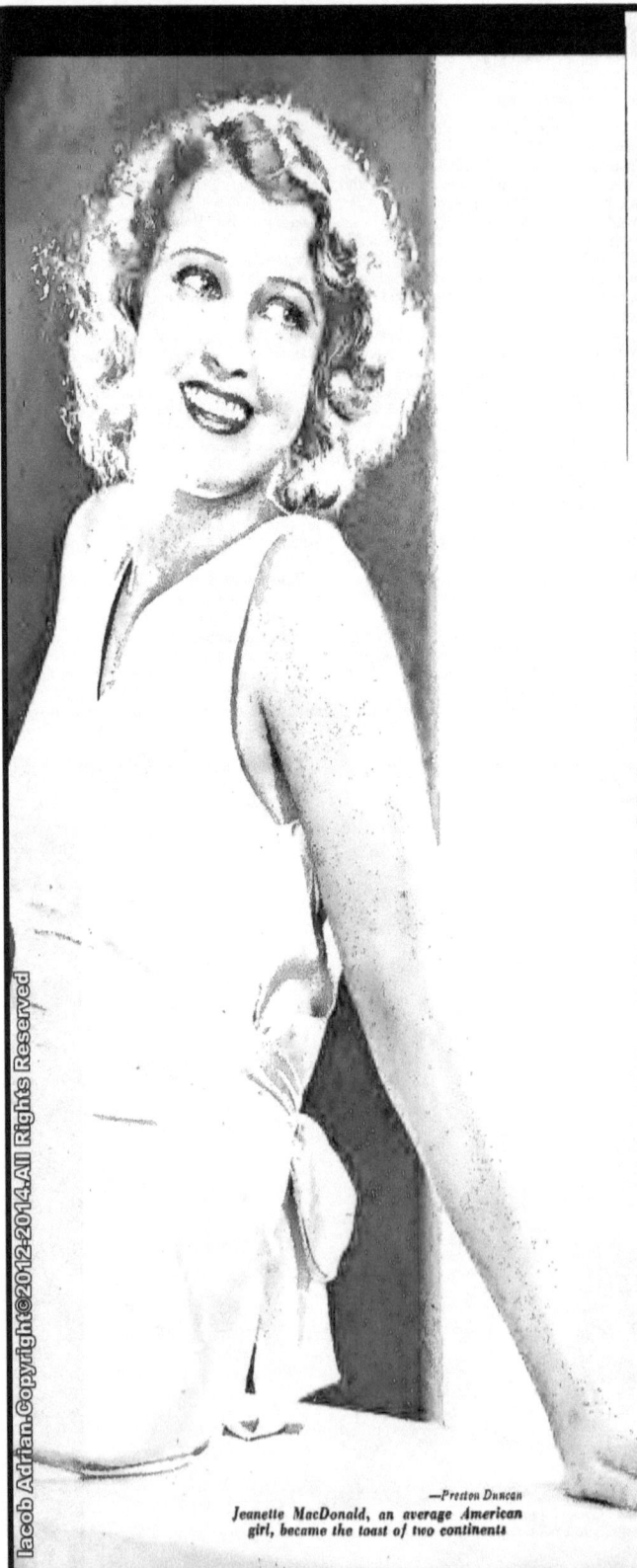

—*Preston Duncan*
Jeanette MacDonald, an average American girl, became the toast of two continents

of the melody came through the loud-speaker; hauntingly beautiful. But what was that? A sour note? Impossible! Then another! And then, ye gods, what a cacophony of discord!

Poor Bela Loblov, a crazed gleam in his eye, tore his hair. He reached for the violin that had betrayed its master, to do violence. Lubitsch laughed and Bela halted. Then he understood—Lubitsch had arranged a fake playback, with some one else playing the melody.

CHEVALIER WAS next on the list of victims. He was talking earnestly with Irving Thalberg when the director sent a boy over to the French star.

"Lubitsch says cut out the gossip; you're wanted on the set," was the message.

"What do you mean?" demanded Chevalier. "Cannot you see I am talking with Mr. Thalberg?"

"Never mind that, come along," said the boy. Then, to escape massacre, he confessed that Lubitsch had put him up to it.

And now for our vengeance. Herr Cupid had things coming to him, and they came.

When the girls in the welcome scene finished lifting Chevalier thirty times, they crept off to conspire. All smeared their lips with all the lipstick they could, inches of it, and ambushed the director. With fiendish cries they sprang, bore him to the ground, and simply covered him with lipstick!

Marcel Achard did not witness it, but he too was avenged. Absent from illness, Lubitsch took his place. The French cast assayed a scene with Lubitsch directing in French. It was a noble effort, but the French that Lubitsch used was like nothing ever heard in Paris. All confused, they halted. Lubitsch glared.

Chevalier stepped up and tapped the maestro gently.

"I did not know, pahdon me," he said, "but are we also making a Chinese version?"

Maurice grinned. He, too, had gotten even. Remained the outraged violinist, and this is what he arranged. Fate played into his hands.

During the picture, Lubitsch is in the habit of passing the time between scenes by playing the piano. He loves to improvise, rambling along on the keys. Sometimes Miss MacDonald sings with him. Bela saw his chance and had the mike swung over the piano getting a recording of Lubitsch.

Time came for the orchestra to record the beautiful Merry Widow waltz. When it was finished, Lubitsch asked for a play-back. A moment of silence, and then the aimless strumming of the maestro at the keyboard greeted him!

Don't get the impression that Lubitsch was neglecting the rôle of cupid. Each day he had some new plan for Miss Mac-Donald's wedding, each more outlandish than the last.

THE GRAND BALL is the pictorial *piece de resistance* of the picture. You stand on the world's largest sound stage, No. 15 on the Metro lot, and a breath-taking vista opens up. The great, circular ball room, giving onto a vast garden promenade to the one side, to the other a huge hall of mirrors that opens to another ballroom and another garden—this one with a real pool flanked by a row of marble statues.

Five hundred extras throng the place

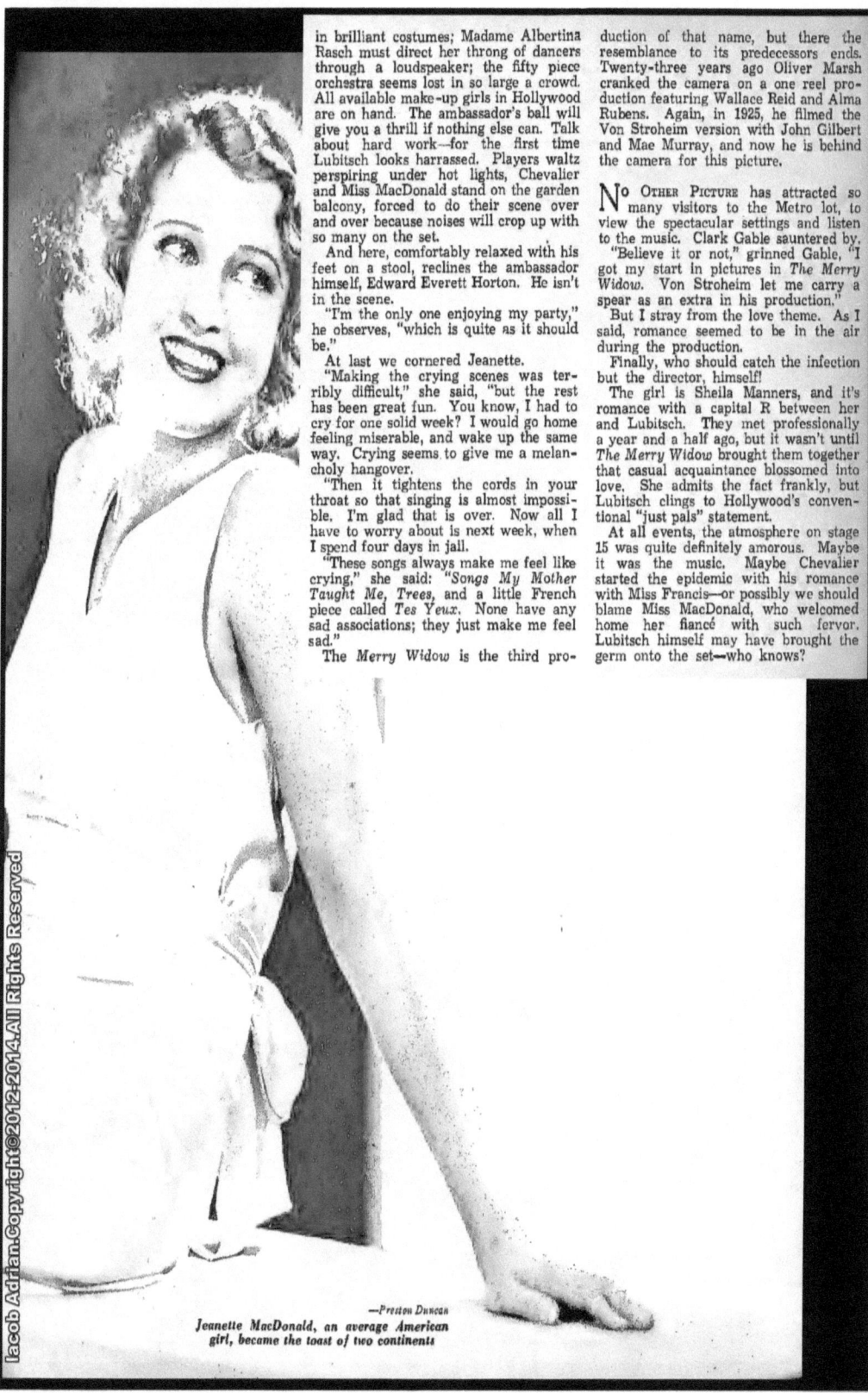

in brilliant costumes; Madame Albertina Rasch must direct her throng of dancers through a loudspeaker; the fifty piece orchestra seems lost in so large a crowd. All available make-up girls in Hollywood are on hand. The ambassador's ball will give you a thrill if nothing else can. Talk about hard work—for the first time Lubitsch looks harrassed. Players waltz perspiring under hot lights, Chevalier and Miss MacDonald stand on the garden balcony, forced to do their scene over and over because noises will crop up with so many on the set.

And here, comfortably relaxed with his feet on a stool, reclines the ambassador himself, Edward Everett Horton. He isn't in the scene.

"I'm the only one enjoying my party," he observes, "which is quite as it should be."

At last we cornered Jeanette.

"Making the crying scenes was terribly difficult," she said, "but the rest has been great fun. You know, I had to cry for one solid week? I would go home feeling miserable, and wake up the same way. Crying seems to give me a melancholy hangover.

"Then it tightens the cords in your throat so that singing is almost impossible. I'm glad that is over. Now all I have to worry about is next week, when I spend four days in jail.

"These songs always make me feel like crying," she said: "Songs My Mother Taught Me, Trees, and a little French piece called Tes Yeux. None have any sad associations; they just make me feel sad."

The Merry Widow is the third production of that name, but there the resemblance to its predecessors ends. Twenty-three years ago Oliver Marsh cranked the camera on a one reel production featuring Wallace Reid and Alma Rubens. Again, in 1925, he filmed the Von Stroheim version with John Gilbert and Mae Murray, and now he is behind the camera for this picture.

No OTHER PICTURE has attracted so many visitors to the Metro lot, to view the spectacular settings and listen to the music. Clark Gable sauntered by.

"Believe it or not," grinned Gable, "I got my start in pictures in The Merry Widow. Von Stroheim let me carry a spear as an extra in his production."

But I stray from the love theme. As I said, romance seemed to be in the air during the production.

Finally, who should catch the infection but the director, himself!

The girl is Sheila Manners, and it's romance with a capital R between her and Lubitsch. They met professionally a year and a half ago, but it wasn't until The Merry Widow brought them together that casual acquaintance blossomed into love. She admits the fact frankly, but Lubitsch clings to Hollywood's conventional "just pals" statement.

At all events, the atmosphere on stage 15 was quite definitely amorous. Maybe it was the music. Maybe Chevalier started the epidemic with his romance with Miss Francis—or possibly we should blame Miss MacDonald, who welcomed home her fiancé with such fervor. Lubitsch himself may have brought the germ onto the set—who knows?

—Preston Duncan

Jeanette MacDonald, an average American girl, became the toast of two continents

Ginger Rogers

A golden gown, say we, is none too good for Ginger —whose glamour, charm, acting and dancing are all of the 22-karat kind. As the pert partner of nimble Fred Astaire, she has become one of the most popular of stars. They'll be together again in *Top Hat!*

Portrait by Ernest Bachrach

Claire Trevor

And ermine is none too good for Claire—who started her screen career as the heroine of a Western and is emerging today as a glamour girl, on the brink of stardom. Her performance as Spencer Tracy's leading lady in *Dante's Inferno* is the tip-off

Portrait by Otto Dyar

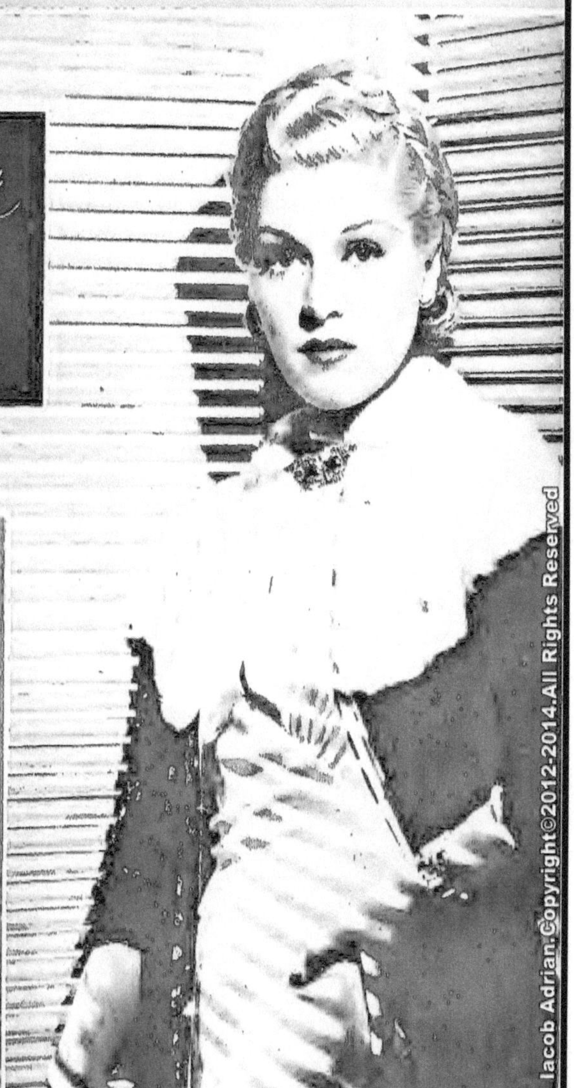

Jeanette MacDonald and Nelson Eddy

All the romance of the New Orleans of 1790, all the charm of Victor Herbert's music—these are what coquettish Jeanette and her new, sensational co-star bring you in *Naughty Marietta*. We warn you: Look and listen for them!

Portrait by C. S. Bull

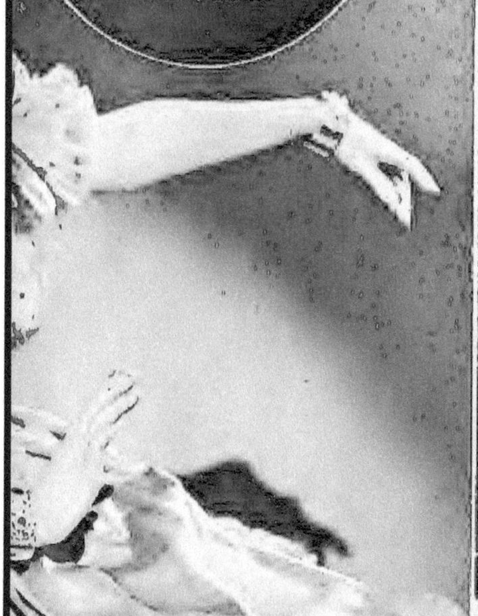

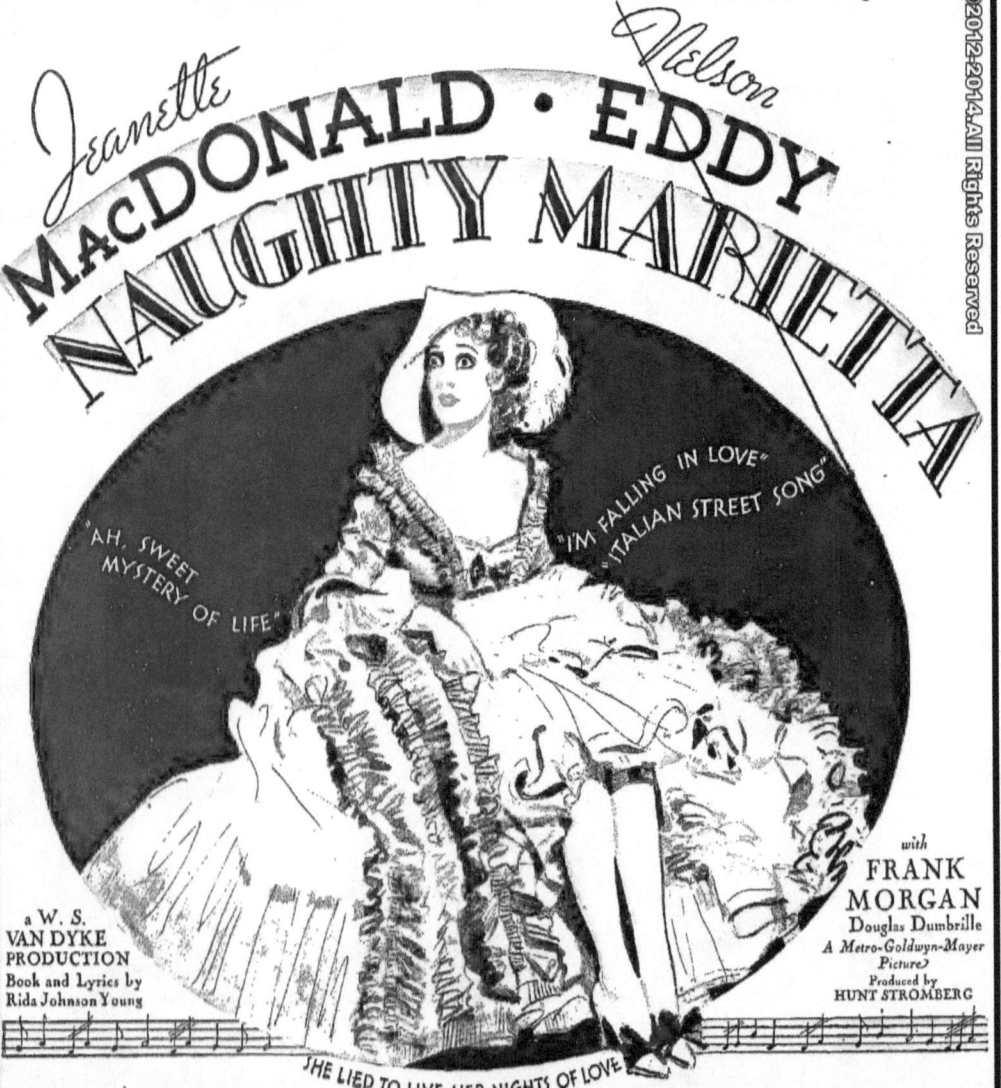

VICTOR HERBERT'S GREATEST—
The BIG MUSICAL OF ALL TIME!

Metro-Goldwyn-Mayer rings up the curtain on its greatest achievement ...a glamorous pageant of drama, mirth and beauty...mightier than any musical yet seen on the screen! You'll thrill to its glittering extravagance...you'll laugh at its bright comedy... and you'll cheer those new sweethearts, Jeanette MacDonald and Nelson Eddy, who found their love under the creole moon. It's the screen's musical masterpiece!

Jeanette MacDONALD • *Nelson* EDDY

NAUGHTY MARIETTA

"AH, SWEET MYSTERY OF LIFE"

"I'M FALLING IN LOVE"

"ITALIAN STREET SONG"

a W. S. VAN DYKE PRODUCTION
Book and Lyrics by Rida Johnson Young

with FRANK MORGAN
Douglas Dumbrille
A Metro-Goldwyn-Mayer Picture
Produced by HUNT STROMBERG

SHE LIED TO LIVE HER NIGHTS OF LOVE

So I'm In Love
with NELSON EDDY!

A brilliant star tells how
romantic rumors start

by

Jeanette MacDonald (signature)

● PERHAPS I SHOULD not be telling this story at all. Doubtless the people who start these absurd rumors of Hollywood romances—and somebody must be the first to gossip—will seize upon my words as new evidence of my "interest" in Nelson Eddy. But I don't mind. We both think it is very funny.

You have heard, of course, that I am "madly in love" with Nelson. That is the reason, they say, my performance in *Naughty Marietta* is "so alive, so fiery, so vibrant." (I am quoting them, you know, and I'm sure I am much obliged. But why, if I gave a good performance, must there be a romantic reason attached?)

I could go on and on for pages about the absurdity of such reports. Just because two people play love scenes on the screen is not an indication that they are in love. Why, I have been forced to kiss men on stage and screen whom I have utterly loathed. It is much more pleasant to play with people you like (remember I said "like"). Yet if you know your business, there is no reason to allow your likes or dislikes to affect your acting.

But I started out to tell you about Nelson Eddy, didn't I? I am sure you will like him. He should become one of the screen's really great stars.

Before we started work together in *Naughty Marietta*, we had met just once or twice casually at the studio. Of course, I knew Nelson Eddy's reputation as one of America's outstanding baritones. But our paths never crossed until we found ourselves both under contract to Metro-Goldwyn-Mayer.

From what he has told me in chats we have had between scenes, I can piece together his life story. I know that he was born in Providence, Rhode Island, and that his father, William Darius Eddy, makes secret devices for Navy submarines. Both his father and mother sing non-professionally.

Nelson's earliest ambition was to be a doctor. Then he decided to become a

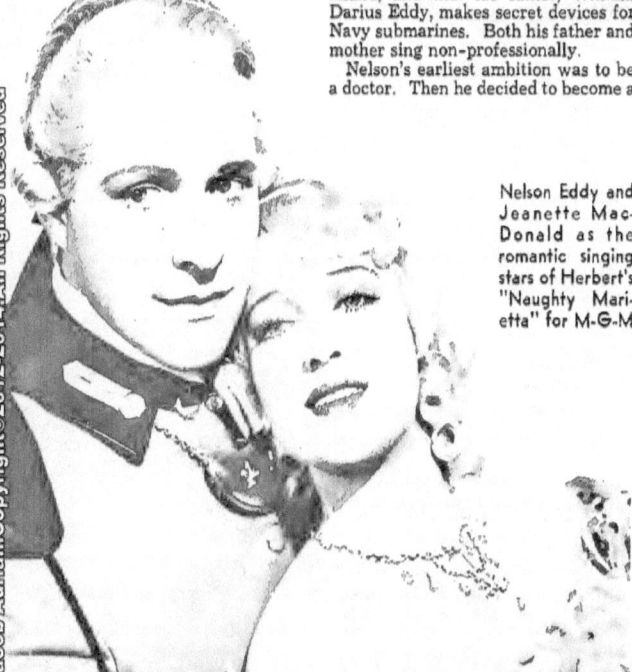

Nelson Eddy and Jeanette Mac-Donald as the romantic singing stars of Herbert's "Naughty Marietta" for M-G-M

trap drummer. His first job, however, was in an iron works.

Very early in life, he discovered his voice. He was—I blush to tell you—a boy soprano.

He sings for the pure joy of singing, and his interest in music has cost him several jobs. Fired by an advertising agency, for which he worked after five years spent as a reporter on Philadelphia newspapers, he signed a radio contract twelve months later with the same agency—at more per week than he earned in a year as a copy reader!

Nelson learned his first arias from phonograph records. Before he had a teacher, he taught himself on the phonograph, playing over and over again the grand opera records by great artists. (Editor's note: Jeanette has neglected to tell you that as a child, she studied the same way.)

● EVEN TODAY, Nelson Eddy works with a phonograph. He has a home recording machine by which he studies his voice, seeking to improve it and adding to his repertoire. He sings thirty-two operatic rôles now.

I've often said that if people are not born with music in their souls, they should not try to sing. If they are born with it, nothing in the world can keep them from singing. Nelson Eddy would have sung whatever his occupation. Being an aggressive chap, he made the sacrifices necessary to carving out a career for himself in music.

This same aggressiveness must have caused his first year in Hollywood to have been literally a torture. Naturally, he was impatient to begin his film work. In a year, he appeared in only two pictures, both small parts.

"I was cast merely because they wanted someone who could sing loud and make gestures," he says now. "And I was handy." But he laughs about it now.

It wasn't that the studio was grooming him for his present stardom. M-G-M knew what he could do. The only difficulty was finding the right story in which he could start. The story finally chosen was *Naughty Marietta*, and I am happy to have been Nelson Eddy's co-star in his début.

Again I say I am sure you will like him.

Strange, I never thought I would like him, myself, judging from our first days on the set. Nelson was very polite —quite too polite. He seemed to avoid speaking to me except when absolutely necessary. I could not understand it.

Then one day, he explained everything. "I've been told that you were an extremely difficult person with whom to work," he said. "You know, prima donna and all that sort of thing. I've been told that you would stoop to anything to steal a scene, and to watch myself. I know now that you have been done an injustice, Jeanette. Will you forgive me?"

That was the beginning of our friendship. You can't help liking such a straight-forward fellow.

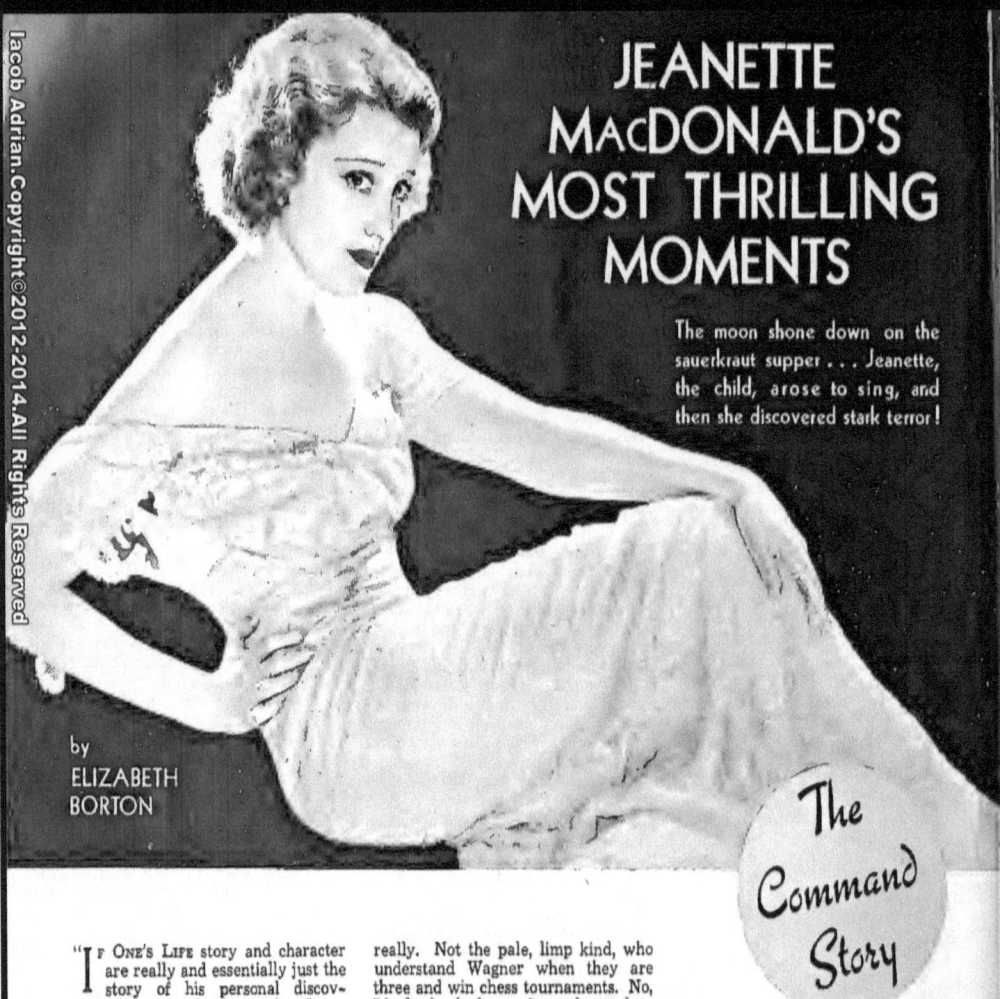

JEANETTE MacDONALD'S MOST THRILLING MOMENTS

The moon shone down on the sauerkraut supper . . . . Jeanette, the child, arose to sing, and then she discovered stark terror!

by
ELIZABETH BORTON

The Command Story

"IF ONE'S LIFE story and character are really and essentially just the story of his personal discoveries, then my life began when I was about four banging on a toy piano on our front porch, with Mr. Natick, the paralyzed man in the wheelchair, on the porch of the adjoining house, looking on," said Jeanette MacDonald.

One of the most versatile and sparkling of cinema's singing actresses, Jeanette, in satin lounging clothes, with the scent of many dozens of cut roses close around her in the warm, luxuriously furnished room, is difficult to associate with the sort of childhood she describes—Elk's suppers at which she sang as a child and sauerkraut high school festivals.

Yet the light of candid humor in her green eyes, her careless sincerity, her laughter—these make you believe her. Besides, there is a sort of detail which marks any story as authentic. So Jeanette MacDonald's account of her personal discoveries is vibrant with truth and with a half-amused, half-tender interest in herself. . . .

"I never made the discovery that I had a voice or could be a singer. I always sang. I was something of a child prodigy . . . not the dreadful kind,

really. Not the pale, limp kind, who understand Wagner when they are three and win chess tournaments. No, I had a fresh clear voice and my adoring older sister taught me, parrot-fashion, to warble things like the 'Jewel Song' from Faust, and 'The Kiss.' I also sang 'John Took Me Round to See His Mother,' and other numbers that the gentlemen used to like. I can see them, clapping, their fat cigars in their

> This Command Story is the editor's compliance to your written demand. Write now, naming your next subject

mouths all the time. I sang for church festivities, and for the Shriners, and the Woodmen of the World. They thought I was wonderful.

"But, I remember so vividly—even before I was a prima donna of eight, in demand at banquets—the moment when I decided that I would be a successful singer. It was on the porch, playing my toy piano. I was singing, and poor Mr. Natick lay with closed eyes in the wheelchair where he lived.

I didn't think it extraordinary that he never walked. I accepted him as he was, inactive, thoughtful—a sort of a man on wheels. Poor soul. My mother came out to shh me. 'You'll bother Mr. Natick,' she said. 'Be quiet.' But he opened his eyes and said to her, 'Oh, let her sing. I like it. And besides, she is going to do things with that singing some day.'"

● AROUND HER As we talked were the clean pale walls of her beautiful living-room. She has recently moved into Brentwood, into a new home. The rose-red carpet threw a glow like firelight into her animated face. Outside the sun shone on the sweep of green lawn and the blue water in her swimming pool.

"Curious, isn't it," she mused, "that I can't remember when my ambition began really, but I can remember Mr. Natick, on the little porch in his chair, and his thin pallid face. . . .

"Little by

Jeanette MacDonald's Thrilling Moments

little, clubs and churches started offering to pay my parents if I would sing. They took the money gladly, putting it into dancing lessons and piano lessons for me. But there was a teacher at school who hated it. She thought I was being exploited. I was always staying out, you see, to sing somewhere, and finally there was an awful day when she sent three people to see us to ask about me. They were Society for the Prevention of Cruelty to Children representatives. I remember them sitting, stiff and disapproving, in our parlor. Mother cried, and I was made to answer questions. That was another discovery for me. I discovered that no one, no matter how smug, can withstand honest, sincere anger. I was only a child, but I knew what their leading questions were for. They were to discredit my mother, to make people think my own darling parents were mean to me.

"Suffice it to say that in the end the report went back to the teacher that the little girl seemed happy in what she was doing, the money was being used for her further training, and she seemed as intelligent and well-informed—with the exception of arithmetic (and they never were able to teach me that!)—as any other little girl in her class.

● "THE NEXT real discovery about myself and my potentialities came tragically. Oh, it may seem funny, young, and naive in the telling—so much is winnowed away in one's memories, and only the essence left—but it was awful! I lost my voice, at the sauerkraut festival. I was to be soloist, and I had practiced and practiced,—a f l o w e r y coloratura number.

My new dress was bouncy with ruffles. Shortly before I had overheard someone say something to indicate that it wasn't, as indeed I had always thought, a shameful burden to go through life with red hair, but something rather intriguing. A boy had said it. I was enchanted. I was happy. I was going to be marvelous at the sauerkraut supper. The moon would shine, I would be lovely in the soft light, everyone would admire me, and my voice would win them. . . .

"But the teacher who had sent the three SPCC people to our house had been invited. As I rose to sing I saw her eyes, scornful and cold, on me. I had the beginning of a sore throat . . . I began to tremble. I started to sing, but my voice wouldn't come. It stopped. There just wasn't anything. Out of pride, I took another number, a simple one, all low notes, and floundered through. I saw her smiling, that teacher, slowly smiling, with triumph at my failure . . . I learned, you see, that I could fail. That it sometimes happened . . . One always has to learn that somewhere along the way."

● HER LITTLE feet, in blue mules, are high-arched, and nervous. She swung one meditatively, thinking of that awful evening in Philadelphia, at the sauerkraut festival . . . She laughed.

"It was later that my older sister went on the stage. After a while, I got a chance. The family had moved to New York, and I had been given dancing lessons for some time. I was terrible at dancing, I thought. They made fun of

me. I couldn't seem to manage the taps. But I labored at it. My voice hadn't come back. It was all I had to do. I worked harder. Finally, I got a job in the chorus. That was the new discovery. There was still another road open to me. I could be a dancer! My voice was gone, but I was paid money, in a show, to dance!

"I was unpopular with the other chorus girls. Maybe because I was younger. Maybe because I gave myself airs. I don't know. Maybe because, after a while, my voice came back, and it seemed better than before! I was allowed to understudy the prima donna. Maybe because I was very conscientious . . . and most of them were not. Anyhow, they let me know that I was not attractive. I heard them saying, 'Some of the most unattractive girls can make themselves up to look grand out front, when the real beauties don't go over . . . Mac, for instance, looks all right . . . out front. . . .'

"But that was another discovery for me. I was used to the fact that I was homely. I had red hair, and light eyebrows and eyelashes, and freckles . . . But I could look lovely out front! With renewed hope, I started learning how. It was not until I saw myself in pictures that I realized that something might be done with this face. . . ."

● THE LOVELY laughing, vivid face, with its shining green eyes, its delicacy of modeling, its frame of shining, curling hair, looks as if it must always have been beautiful.

"I remember that the only pleasant memory of my appearance I ever had, up to the time I saw my first screen test, was when a teacher went bouncing round our room one time, looking at heads. You know . . . one little girl had been discovered . . . with . . . things . . . in her hair. Round went the teacher, looking with chilled apprehension at all the little skulls. She looked at me. 'Lovely,' she said. 'Lovely hair and scalp. Nice child.' She patted me. I hugged those words to me for a long time. They were the nearest I ever got to a compliment on my looks, until that boy said, 'Ummmm, a redhead,' with frank admiration as I went by, and something deep and instinctive told me that it was all right, that I didn't have to defy people about my hair any more.

"Then came a r e a l discovery—an enormously important one. I started going to symphony concerts whenever I could, and good recitals—largely to keep up a superior pose of being really musical in front of the other girls in the show.

"Then one day, I heard Toscanini conduct a Beethoven symphony, and suddenly the whole world went round and everything fell away except the music and the magnificence of the emotions within it. I cried. I was terribly embarrassed, but excited and transfigured. I hadn't been unhappy. It was no personal emotion which swept me. It was something outside, something abstract, and yet it touched things in me deeper than anything I had ever felt before.

"I learned what music was. Music had always been something nice, sweet, pleasant before. . . . something I could do, and people admired me for it. But this was the revelation to me of what music was and would mean. I have never been able

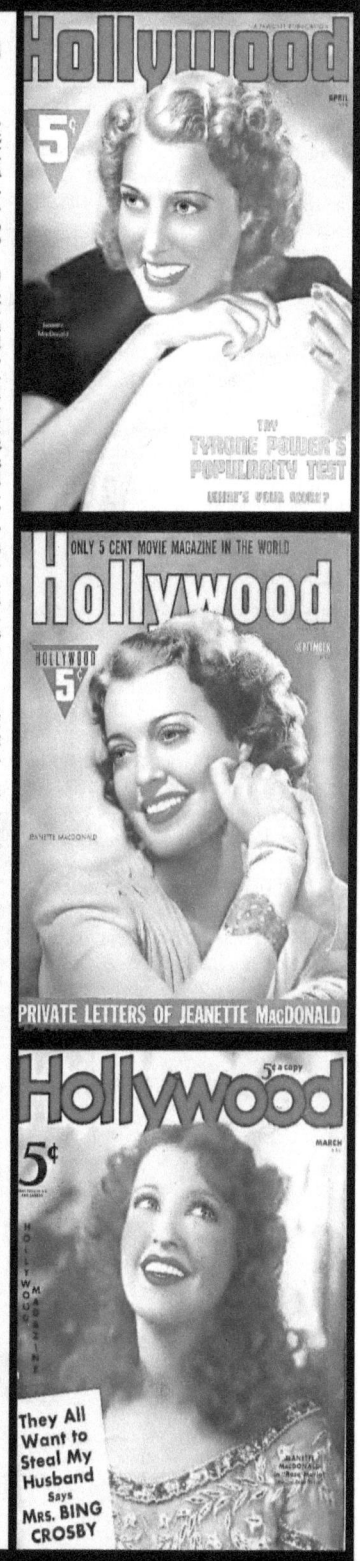

to do without it since. It changed me completely . . . musically, I grew up.

"Another discovery was that, in order to express my deepest feelings, I must learn to feel them less . . . No one can sing if he is really personally sad. The muscles of the throat tighten, the chords relax.

"And, of course, love. Love is the discovery that is always new. No two people ever feel just like any other two. I was tremendously affected by falling in love. The personal discoveries I made during that time of glow and breathless happiness and excitement, I cherish. But the greatest discovery, for me, was that this lovely thing, which all girls dream of so hopefully, which every woman waits for, once achieved, is not like a bird caught, or a treasure found.

"It is a vital, struggling thing, evanescent, intangible. It slips away as suddenly as it comes. Suddenly, it is simply gone, and the moment any woman discovers this—not the man doesn't love her any more (that is a discovery women steel themselves to cope with, it is so expected, in a buried sort of way, in every man and woman relationship)—but that she herself, for no reason she can name, simply doesn't love any more, her faith in herself is rocked.

◉ "SHE UNDERGOES self-distrust, fear . . . Her personal securities are shaken, for of all people from whom we expect certain definite things and reactions, you know, ourselves are dearest to us . . . I learned that I could love, and that also love could vanish from my heart and life . . . Well, the discovery is a great teacher. . . .

"I have never experienced what is for most women the supreme personal discovery . . . motherhood. I can't, because I have decided definitely against marriage, and for a career . . . Marriage is a career for a woman, and she has to have certain special talents to be successful at it. I'm already started at another career. I'm not so egotistical as to think I can simply swap and be as successful in one as the other. I know how hard it is to make a success of any career. I know my limitations. . . .

"I shan't regret not undergoing the physical functions of motherhood, though, because it is still possible for me to take over the psychological ones. I can adopt a child, and I shall.

"Some day I shall go to an orphanage and I shall look at all the little children. But not to pick out the prettiest, the cutest, the one with dimples, and curls, and cute ways. I shall choose the little one that is pale and resigned, the one who isn't pretty or talented, the one nobody else wants, the one who has long since given up the hope that some day a mama and papa will come for him. . . .

"Then I'll see what love and hope and fun and help can do for a child . . . Then I'll open up for both of us a new world of discoveries. . . ."

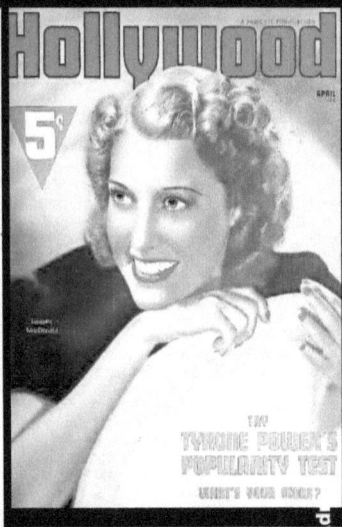

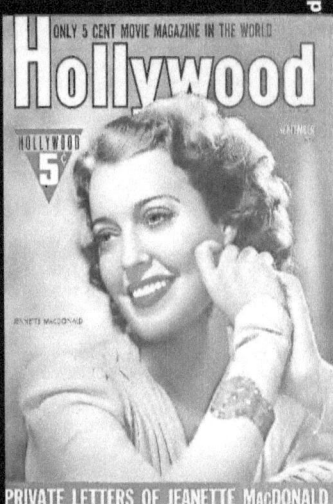

PRIVATE LETTERS OF JEANETTE MacDONALD

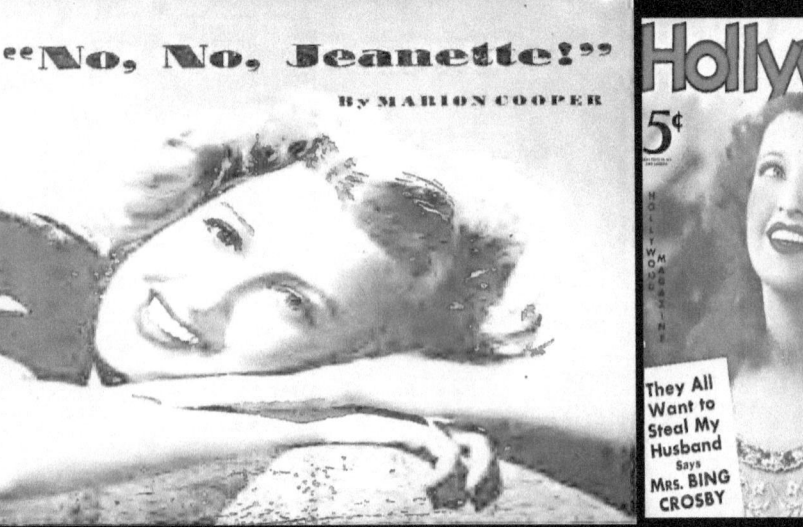

"No, No, Jeanette!"

By MARION COOPER

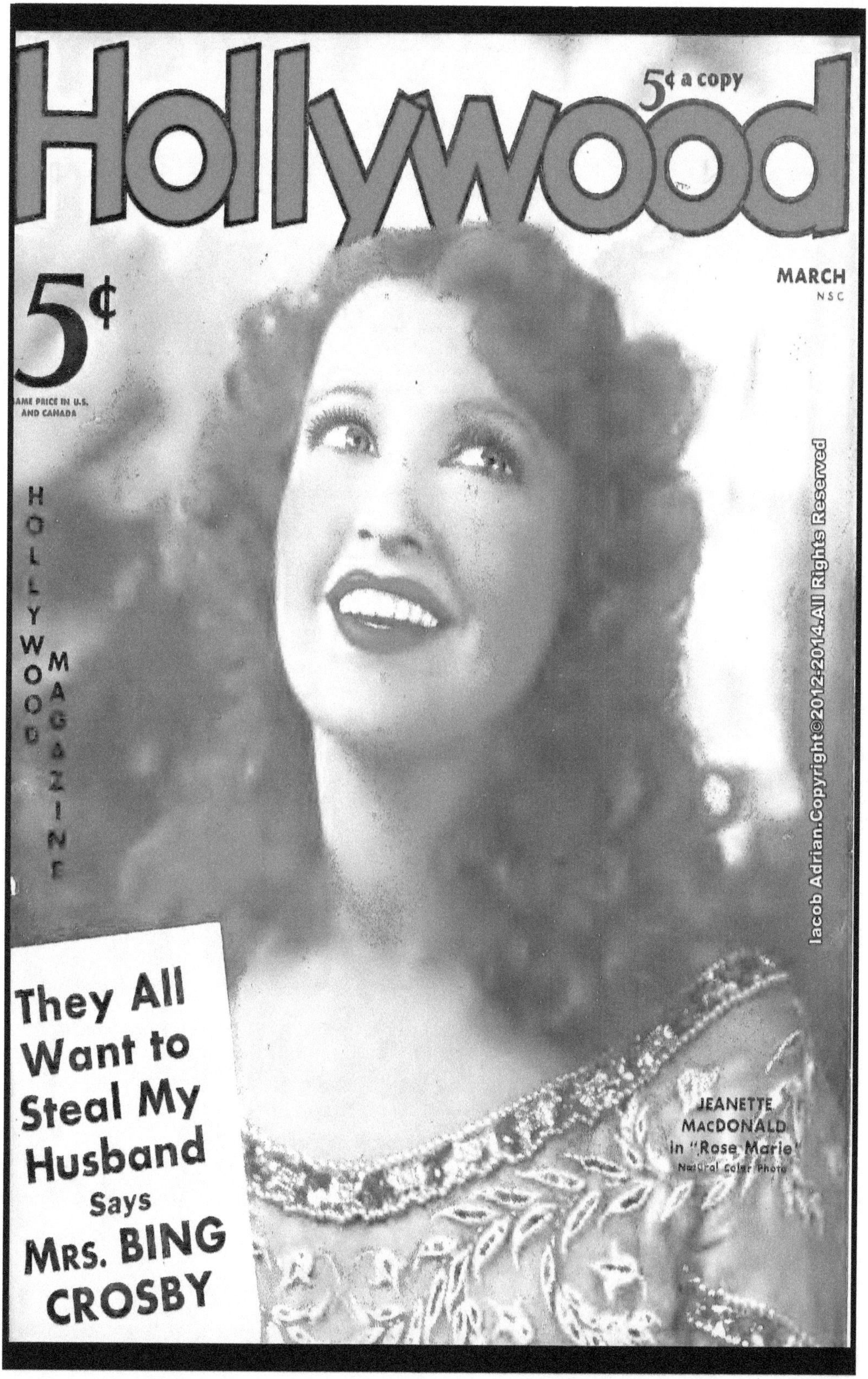

Hollywood

5¢ a copy

5¢

SAME PRICE IN U.S.
AND CANADA

HOLLYWOOD MAGAZINE

They All
Want to
Steal My
Husband
Says
MRS. BING
CROSBY

JEANETTE
MacDONALD
in "Rose-Marie"
Natural Color Photo

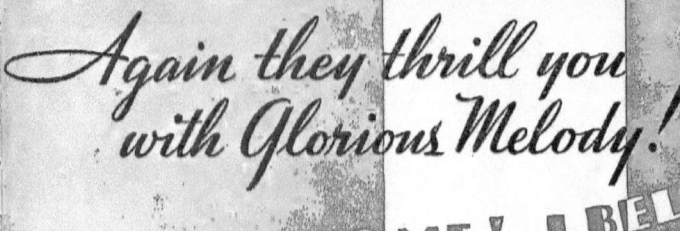

Again they thrill you with Glorious Melody!

"YOU BELONG TO ME! I BELONG TO YOU"

The singing stars of "Naughty Marietta" now lift their golden voices to excite all the world with the immortal melodies of the most vibrant and stirring musical of our time — "Rose Marie"... The romantic drama of a pampered pet of the opera and a rugged "Mountie" torn between love and duty, whose hearts' met where mountains touched the sky...How you'll thrill with delight as they fill the air with your love songs — "Rose Marie, I Love You", and "Indian Love Call"! It's the first big musical hit of 1936—another triumph for the M-G-M studios!

Thrill to Jeanette MacDonald as she sings "The Waltz Song" from Romeo and Juliet, and with Nelson Eddy, the immortal duet "Indian Love Call"

Jeanette
Mac DONALD
NELSON EDDY
IN
Rose Marie

'SONG OF THE MOUNTIES!' 300 rugged male voices led by Nelson Eddy in the most stirring song of our time!

A Metro-Goldwyn-Mayer Picture
with
REGINALD OWEN · ALLAN JONES
Directed by W. S. Van Dyke · Produced by Hunt Stromberg

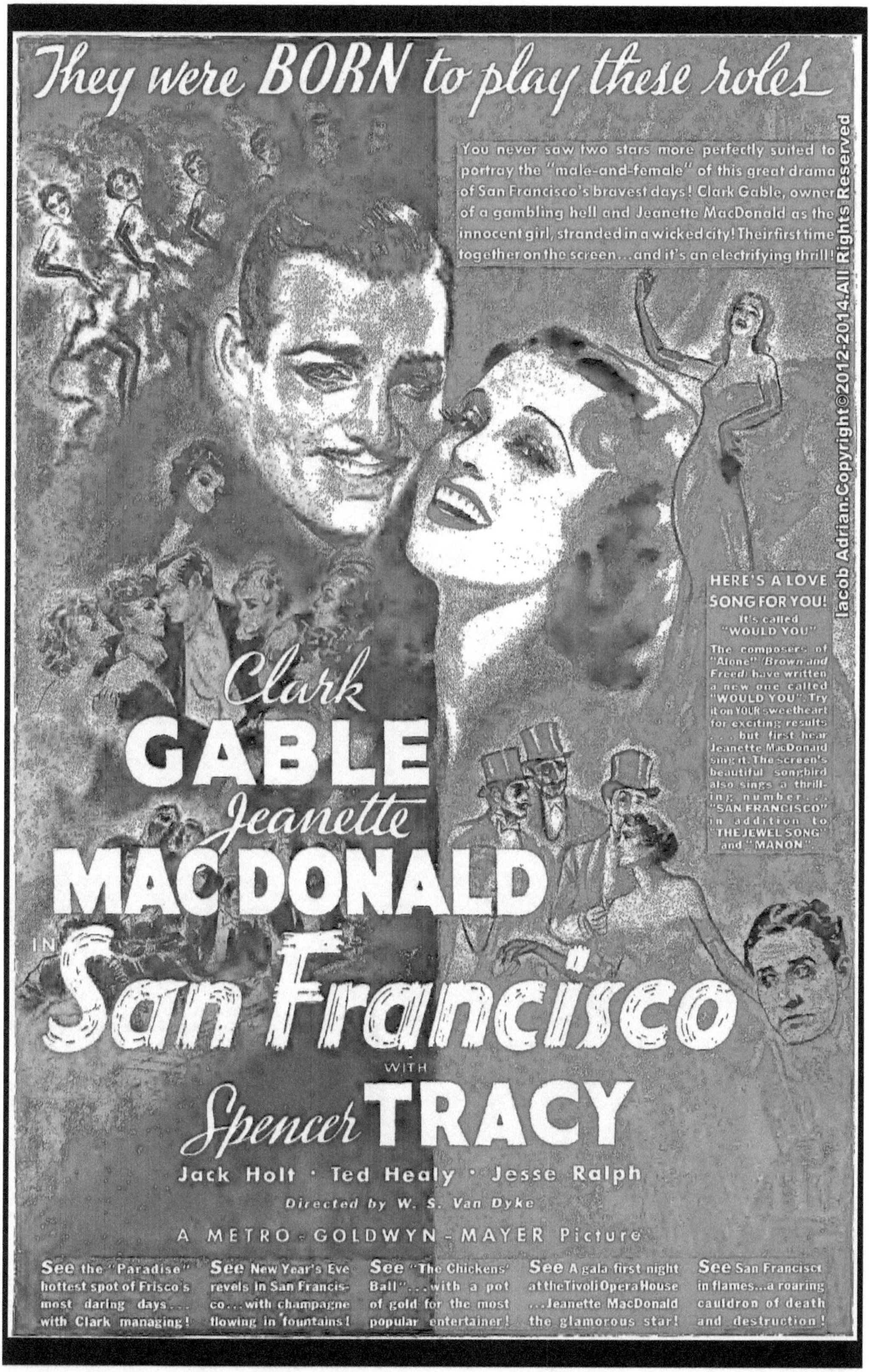

They were BORN to play these roles

You never saw two stars more perfectly suited to portray the "male-and-female" of this great drama of San Francisco's bravest days! Clark Gable, owner of a gambling hell and Jeanette MacDonald as the innocent girl, stranded in a wicked city! Their first time together on the screen...and it's an electrifying thrill!

HERE'S A LOVE SONG FOR YOU!
It's called "WOULD YOU"
The composers of "Alone" Brown and Freed have written a new one called "WOULD YOU". Try it on YOUR sweetheart for exciting results ...but first hear Jeanette MacDonald sing it. The screen's beautiful songbird also sings a thrilling number... "SAN FRANCISCO" in addition to "THE JEWEL SONG" and "MANON".

Clark
GABLE
Jeanette
MAC DONALD
in
San Francisco
with
SPENCER TRACY

Jack Holt · Ted Healy · Jesse Ralph
Directed by W. S. Van Dyke
A METRO - GOLDWYN - MAYER Picture

See the "Paradise" hottest spot of Frisco's most daring days... with Clark managing!

See New Year's Eve revels in San Francisco...with champagne flowing in fountains!

See "The Chickens' Ball"...with a pot of gold for the most popular entertainer!

See A gala first night at the Tivoli Opera House ...Jeanette MacDonald the glamorous star!

See San Francisco in flames...a roaring cauldron of death and destruction!

My Daughter, Jeanette MacDonald
by
Mrs. Anna MacDonald

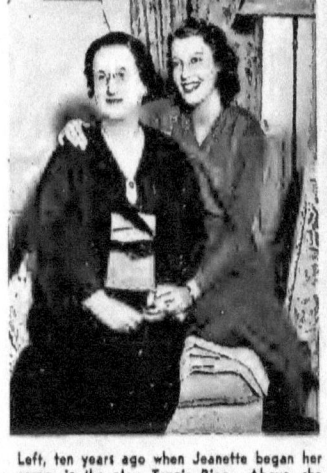

Left, ten years ago when Jeanette began her career in the play, *Tragic Ring*. Above, she is shown with her mother, who often accompanies her around Hollywood

JEANETTE MacDONALD's performance in *San Francisco* has pleased us all. I am proud of my daughter for her fine work. I think the studio is equally proud. So naturally I am glad to tell the readers of HOLLYWOOD Magazine the story of our lives together in the years gone by.

Everything happens for the best. That old saying has been in our family for a long, long time. It's a sort of whistle in the dark to keep up courage. We apply it when anything happens that we didn't expect to happen and it seems to exonerate us from any blame as to the outcome.

My two oldest daughters, Elsie and Blossom, were no longer babies and I was just breathing a sigh of relief over my lessened responsibilities as a mother when I discovered that my family was not yet completed. But I simply applied the old adage, *everything happens for the best,* and began making plans for the new baby.

Jeanette was a darling baby—big-eyed and of sunny disposition. Oh, she wasn't too good to be true—she managed to get into enough mischief so that we were well aware of her existence.

When most babies her age were crying she was singing. She had a toy piano and she would sit on the porch and play it and sing by the hour to her grandfather —and to the neighbors.

Singing from a Swing

● I USED TO TAKE HER over to the childrens' playground in the park so that she might take advantage of the sand boxes and the swings. One day when she was a little past two years old, she climbed up in one of the swings and began singing

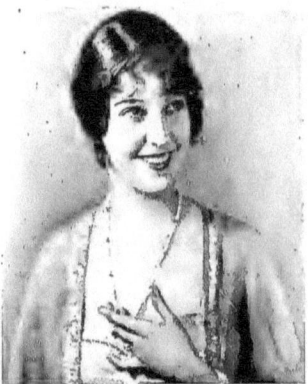

at the top of her voice. I imagine that she fancied herself a prima donna and the other children her audience.

The care-taker asked me how old she was and when I told him he shook his head and said, "Well, I've been here a long time and I've seen plenty of them sing but I never saw such a little one sing and never heard anyone sing so loud."

He took her over to his house and made a record of her singing. Voice recording was not the art then that it is today but the reproduction wasn't bad. Years later we tried to locate that record but it had been broken.

Elsie and Blossom were both very interested in Jeanette's voice. They had reached the age when they were anxious to impart a bit of the knowledge they had learned and

Jeanette was a good subject. Elsie would play the piano and Jeanette would sit beside her and sing, never failing to ask what the words meant and inventing gestures to go with them.

Elsie now has a school in the East where she instructs children and says that she got the idea of such a school from the memory of her lessons to Jeanette.

Outside of singing at every excuse she could find or invent, Jeanette was a very normal little girl. She went to public school and received all the praise and scoldings that her classmates received.

Pickles and Weight

● SHE NEVER WAS a tale-bearer so perhaps she figured in a few childish escapades that I never knew about. Just the other day she told me that she used to take part of her lunch money every day and buy a big sour pickle and eat it on the way to school.

Elsie eloped from school and married— Blossom was working in Ned Weyburn's *Demi-Tasse Revue* at the Capitol Theatre and little Jeanette felt herself pretty much left out of things—a failure at fourteen.

To add a little sparkle to the dull routine of her life, her father took her to New York and left her at the theatre with Blossom while he attended to some business.

Jeanette made very good use of her time at the theatre. Mr. Weyburn told her that she could appear in the revue as a chorus girl and under-study one of the principals.

She knew she would meet opposition to her plans when she reached home so she figured out just what our objections would be and was ready with a refutation for every objection.

She was too young to be away from home.

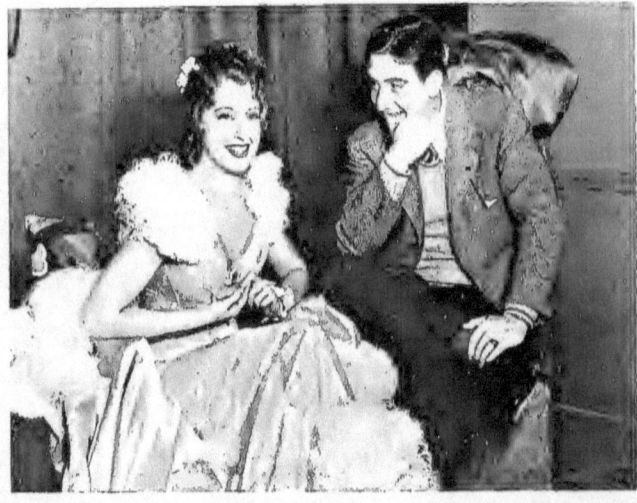

In M-G-M's film, *San Francisco*, Jeanette MacDonald scores the greatest personal triumph of her career. Here she is shown with Spencer Tracy in an off-stage scene. He plays the rôle of a prelate

My Daughter, Jeanette MacDonald

"But I won't be among strangers—I'll be with Blossom."

She couldn't give up school at fourteen.

"But I won't have to give up school. I can go in New York. Mr. Weyburn will make arrangements with the principal so that I can be excused for a matinee on Wednesday."

Her music—she must not sacrifice that either.

"Oh no, indeed! There is a piano backstage and I can practice there just the same as if I were right at home."

A Career at Fourteen

● No MATTER WHAT objection I raised, she had it over-ruled. I asked her father and, like most fathers where girls are concerned, he left the matter up to me. I didn't want to be a foolish mother and stand in her way—maybe this *was* an opportunity—surely she must have something or she would not have been *offered* a chance when so many girls were *begging* for one.

I finally let her go. She kept her word about school and her music lessons. From that time on her rise has been gradual but sure. She studied hard and worked hard and she still does. Every day she is not working, she takes a voice lesson—and sometimes when she is working if she can steal an hour from the set.

She studies piano also—not that she ever expects to make professional use of the knowledge, but because she enjoys it.

Jeanette had played in *Yes, Yes Yvette*. It was purchased as a talking vehicle for Richard Dix, to be screened under the title of *Nothing But the Truth*. Jeanette was tested for the feminine lead but her manager would not permit her to accept film work. She was disappointed but resorted to the old form of courage—*everything happens for the best*—and in this case, it did.

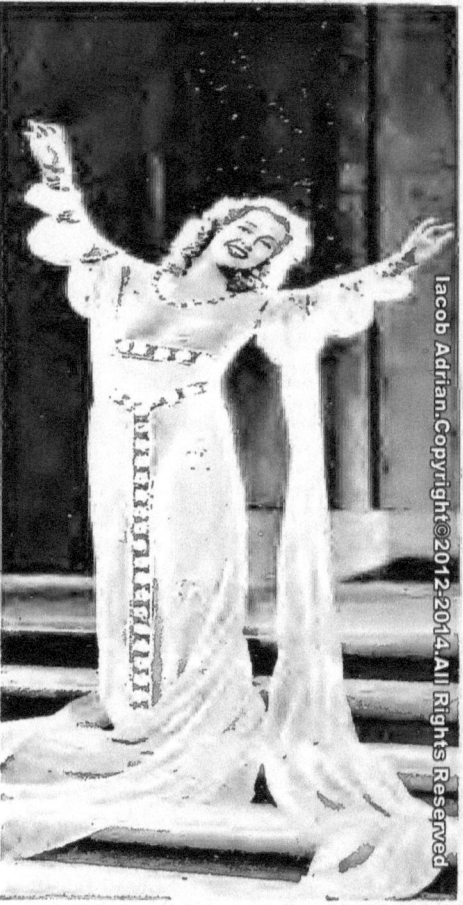

In *Rose Marie*, currently being shown everywhere, Jeanette plays the rôle of an opera singer in love with a Mountie. This is a scene from her *Romeo and Juliet* number

She Enters Films

● THE ROLE OPPOSITE Mr. Dix did not amount to very much. It was a straight part and would not have permitted Jeanette to use her talent as a singer. Six months later when Mr. Lubitsch was looking for a girl to play opposite Maurice Chevalier in *The Love Parade*, he looked at that old test and sent for Jeanette.

That was in 1929—since that time she has been working in pictures steadily except for a concert tour through Europe.

Jeanette has always been a very busy person. She seldom takes time to rest or to thoroughly enjoy the profits of her success. She is forever trying to perfect something, or to learn something new. She does enjoy her swimming pool. She also enjoys tennis but doesn't play as much as she would like simply because she never had time to perfect her game and she isn't the sort to do anything unless she can do it well.

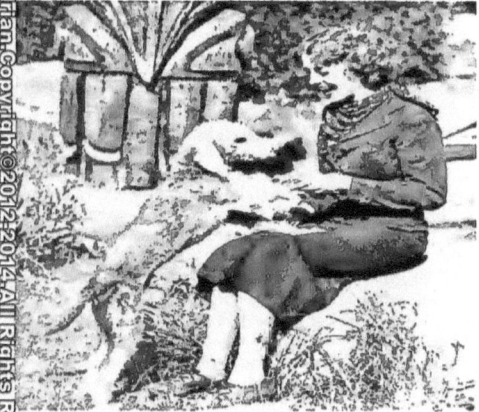

This strange dog is a Bedlington Terrier named *Piper*, brought to Jeanette MacDonald by Robert Ritchie, her business manager. Romance rumors about them are all in error. The real lad is Gene Raymond

DOES HOLLYWOOD

Defy

ROMANCE?

By CHARLES DARNTON

WITH marriage bells on her tongue, it was only fitting that the melodious Jeanette MacDonald should have rings on her fingers, among them one of the engagement variety which gives sparkle to romance.

Yet its fair wearer sat there in sunlight like part of her luminous hair and jealously guarded her romance with Gene Raymond.

"I'm superstitious about it," she hesitated to say.

There was no mistaking the dread in her voice. But it was not so readily understood. To be sure, a bride-elect might well be superstitious about a rainy wedding day, or as to wearing something old, something new, something borrowed, something blue. Call this superstition if you like, though it's really tradition. Anyway, it has nothing to do with actual fear. Of what, for that matter, had Miss MacDonald to be afraid?

"Hollywood," was her definite reply. "It defies romance. Now you might think, since its screen aspect is largely concerned with romance, that Hollywood would be sympathetic toward it. But the opposite is true where individuals are concerned. I'm willing to grant that an attempt, often successful, is made to have it appear that two stars are romantically interested in each other, but as a rule this is wholly a matter of box-office business. Really, Hollywood is utterly merciless in its defiance of romance."

Hearing was believing this, for it carried the conviction of brains. That pretty head of hers was packed with them, that blue eye of hers flashed with intelligence. Yet there was a

Why is Hollywood the most difficult of all places for romance? Why have so many film careers been wrecked because of love? Sensible, practical, and beautiful Jeanette MacDonald, whose marriage to Gene Raymond is scheduled for June will surprise you with her answers to these questions

—*Photograph by Clarence Bull*

Heroine of M-G-M's Maytime is golden-voiced Jeanette MacDonald who co-stars with Nelson Eddy in an elaborate cast

great deal to be explained. Nothing could have done it more clearly than:

"Unusual circumstances, peculiar conditions which exist nowhere else, make Hollywood the most difficult of all places for romance. Unfortunately, we can't keep it to ourselves for the simple reason that we are public property. That's what we're up against in Hollywood. Everything we do is universally known. This is only natural, and there's no defense against it. The very fact that our faces are known everywhere makes the public feel it really knows us. We are known not just as names but as personalities. So

we can't really blame them for feeling as they do about us. We work on their imaginations and play on their emotions so largely that they feel they know what ours are like. Of course they don't, but this doesn't help us. We just have to make the best of what doesn't show inside us and what does show outside. We have to watch ourselves every minute, because we are constantly watched. Why, if we put on even an added pound of weight it's noticed.

"At any rate, I don't have to worry about that. While others are in a

• Does Hollywood Defy Romance? •

furor to get thin, I'm trying to gain weight."

By way of illustration the smilingly immune prima donna of *Maytime* plumped a spot of jelly on her daily bread.

"**F**AT or lean," she blithely went on, "is merely a matter of fashion. I don't think romance enters into it at all.

"No, I've never been in love with my leading man. Some say you must 'live' your role. But Sarah Bernhardt said the audience, not the player, should live it, and I've always believed she was right.

"What can be done to help Hollywood romance," pointed out Miss MacDonald, "is to give it a finer understanding than can be gained from the mere excitement of it. Excitement should, and no doubt does, make the actor and actress more nervous than usual, and it has been said that the more highly strung they are the better their performance. But this may also have a disturbing effect. And I see no reason why having love in one's life should interfere with one's work. After all, doesn't a man say to the woman he loves that she will be an inspiration to his work? Well, this is just as true of a woman. It gives her something more than she has had, a fuller life. What romance means most of all is escape from loneliness, something to fill the emptiness of life. It is this same need which accounts for the success of all the arts—painting, music, drama and others—bringing with them as they do moments of forgetfulness and taking us away from ourselves."

DANCING with the sunbeams through her hair seemed to be impish spirits whose antic capers suggested that romance itself might be a fleeting thing.

"Love can't last," Miss MacDonald was quick to say, "if you haven't the mentality to make it last. A person without the thought and care which love deserves and requires is not intelligent enough to make it survive. But the mischief doesn't always stop there. Romance may wreck a career, especially in Hollywood. But this is true only when the individual lets romance control and dominate his life and work. Then it means the tossing away of his career. It is unwise to stake all you have on love. Nor do I think it was ever intended that love should be everything in life to us, for in that case work wouldn't enter into the

scheme of things. I place everything I hope to get out of life, on an equal basis. Unfortunately, this is not an easy thing to do in Hollywood. Here one's judgment is influenced by considering what people will say. Now there are people who say you can't live without love. But what I say is you can't live on love. With or without it, you must have work. I've no patience with people who talk of the suffering they endure and the sacrifice they make because of their work. I always pooh-pooh those who say this in Hollywood. If they don't want to work they can give it up. For my part, I like it. And I'm frank to admit that one of the nicest things about work is the pay check."

THERE was no pooh-poohing the sensible, practical Miss MacDonald on this subject, for she went to work at an early age and has been at it ever since. "There's a feeling of keen satisfaction in it," she admitted. "I still get a bit of a thrill when I see a presentation on the stage of a movie theater and wonder which one of those girls in the chorus line will work her way out of it into something better some day. It always takes me back to the day in New York when I started at fourteen in the chorus at the Capitol Theater. If anyone had told me then that I would ever appear on the screen of that theater I'd probably have dropped with surprise. At that time Hollywood might just as well have been in another world. But I must say that since coming here to be with Maurice Chevalier in *The Love Parade* it has been a workaday world for me. The most difficult thing for me up to that time was my reputation as a dancer. I loathed it, for it meant that no one probably would ever take my singing seriously. But I must admit that dancing served me very well—got me a job and paid the rent. Singing was always secondary till I got into pictures."

That was six years ago. But apparently she was thinking not of herself but of the place to which she had come.

"What was true of Hollywood then is still true," she reflected, "only now it is a little worse. By this I don't mean its work, but its interference in private lives. In this respect it is more brazen, its remarks are less veiled. But the shafts which are so deadly to romance come for the most part from outside. We are natural targets. Set up as we are in the public eye, this is only inevitable. Yet Mrs. Vandergilt might say, 'You should live in *my* circle!' And it's all very well to talk about

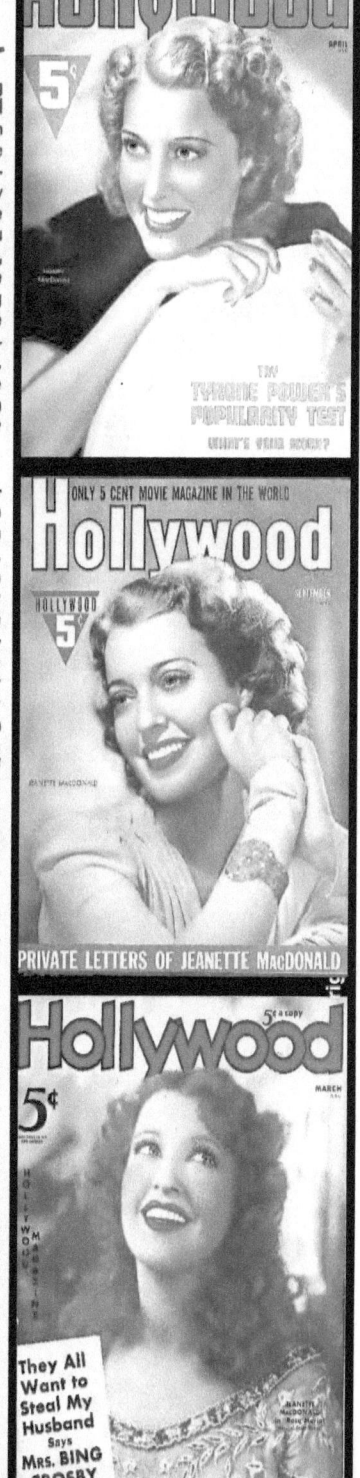

Mrs. Brownington Jones, but that talk is never heard outside her own neighborhood. Hollywood talk goes 'round the world."

Miss MacDonald knitted her brows over the problem, only to challenge it with:

"When I read Hollywood scandal I always give it the benefit of the doubt. But it can't be denied there's no way to avoid speculation, and it's awful to be the subject of speculation. There's no defense against it. All you can do is lead a conservative, decent life and hope it will be taken for what it is. Truth is the only thing that counts. But when a wrong impression is created it may prevail even against truth. Malicious gossip can ruin a life. And nowhere is this quite so true as in Hollywood, where gossip is published. There may be just as many marriages, divorces and scandals in other parts of the world, but in Hollywood they are more publicized, and not through any desire on the part of individuals involved. Now a Hollywood actress may want privacy just as much as Mrs. John Smith, but she doesn't get it.

"But understand me, I feel very kindly toward Hollywood. It has given me position, financial status and a

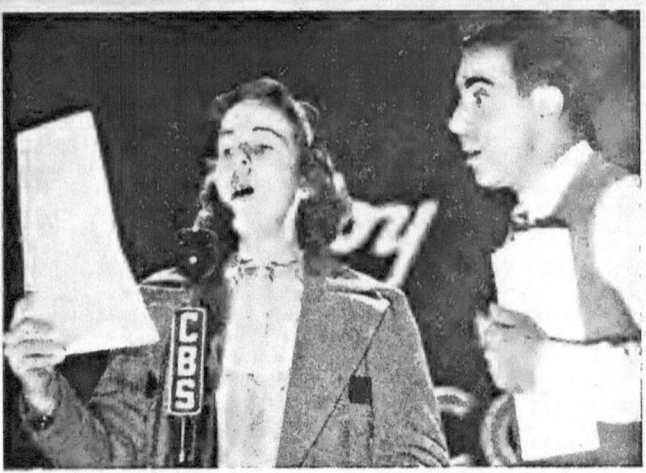

Deanna Durbin is doing the singing, but Eddie Cantor works just as hard listening, unless the candid camera made a mistake

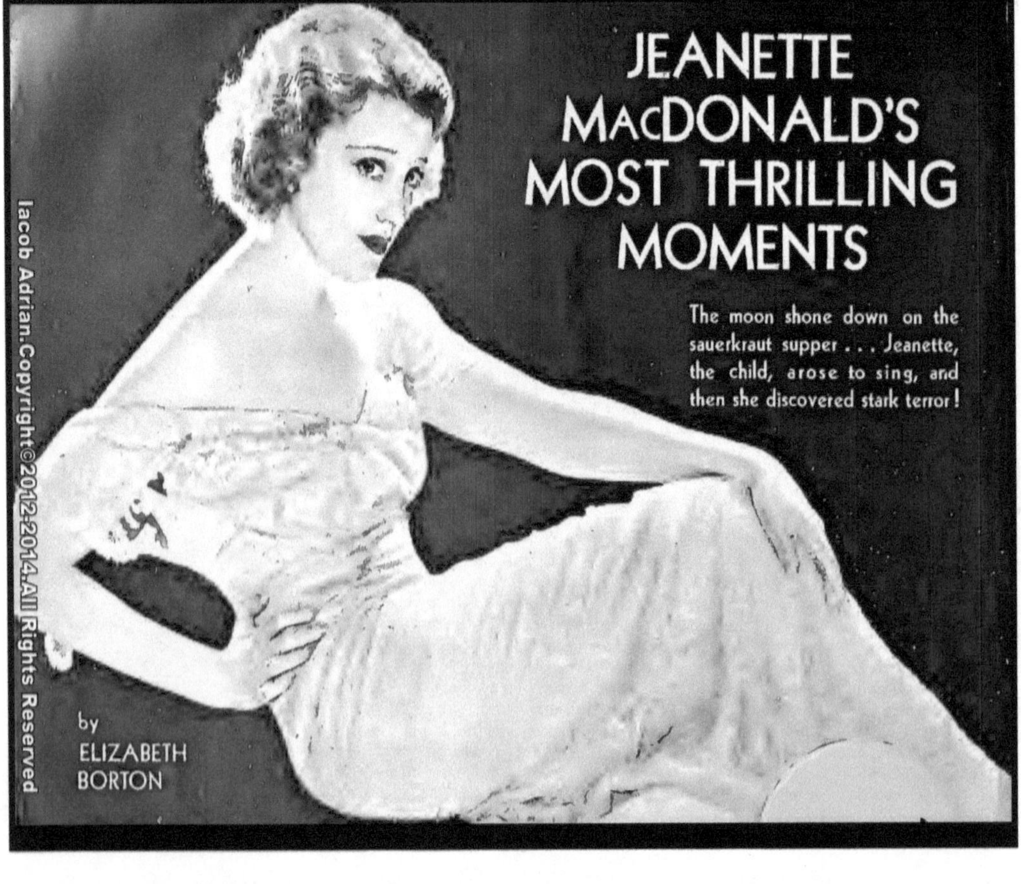

place to work. For all this I am very grateful. I want to get everything possible out of life and work out my own destiny. But here things are so contingent on one another that this is hard to do. When romance enters into Holly-

wood life nothing could be harder. No matter. I've never been easily frightened. And now Hollywood, with all its defiance of romance, can't scare me out of mine."

Of course not. It's the Scotch in her!

JEANETTE MacDONALD'S MOST THRILLING MOMENTS

The moon shone down on the sauerkraut supper . . . Jeanette, the child, arose to sing, and then she discovered stark terror!

by
ELIZABETH
BORTON

Wedding
of the SEASON

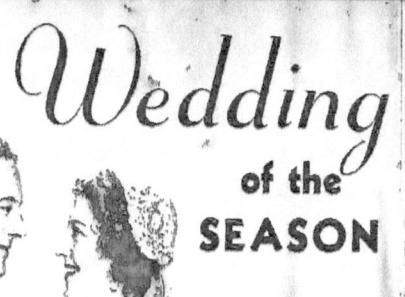

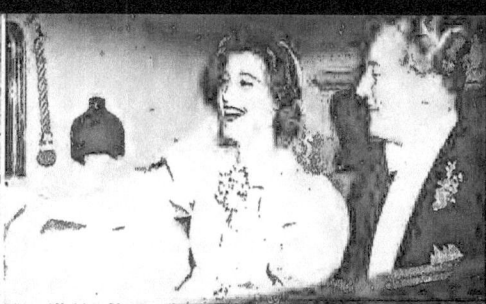

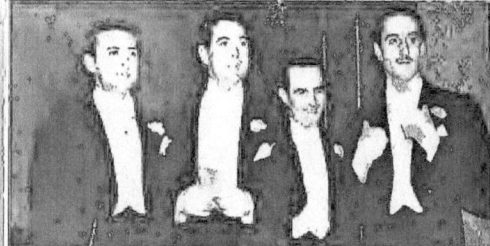

Ushers were Allan Jones, John Mack Brown, Harold Lloyd and Basil Rathbone

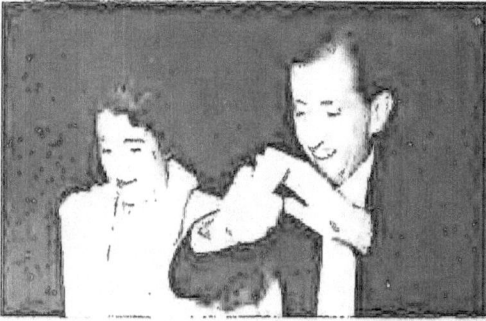

Mr. and Mrs. Will Hays. The film czar is not offering a prayer; merely signalling cameramen to cease "shooting"
—Fawcett candid photos by Rhodes

Gene Raymond and Jeanette MacDonald photographed of the church after marriage vows were taken

Exclusive HOLLYWOOD Portrait by Hale

(Bottom, right) The bridal group: Helen Ferguson, Mrs. Warren Rock (sister of the bride), the bride, the groom, Fay Wray, Ginger Rogers and Mr. John Mack Brown

Fawcett photo by Rhodes

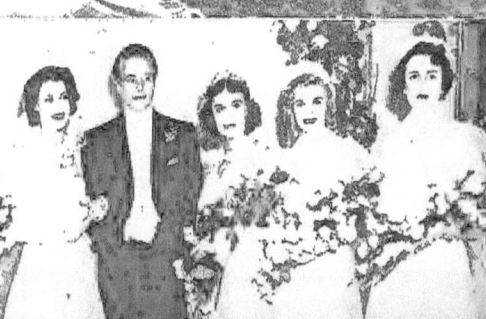

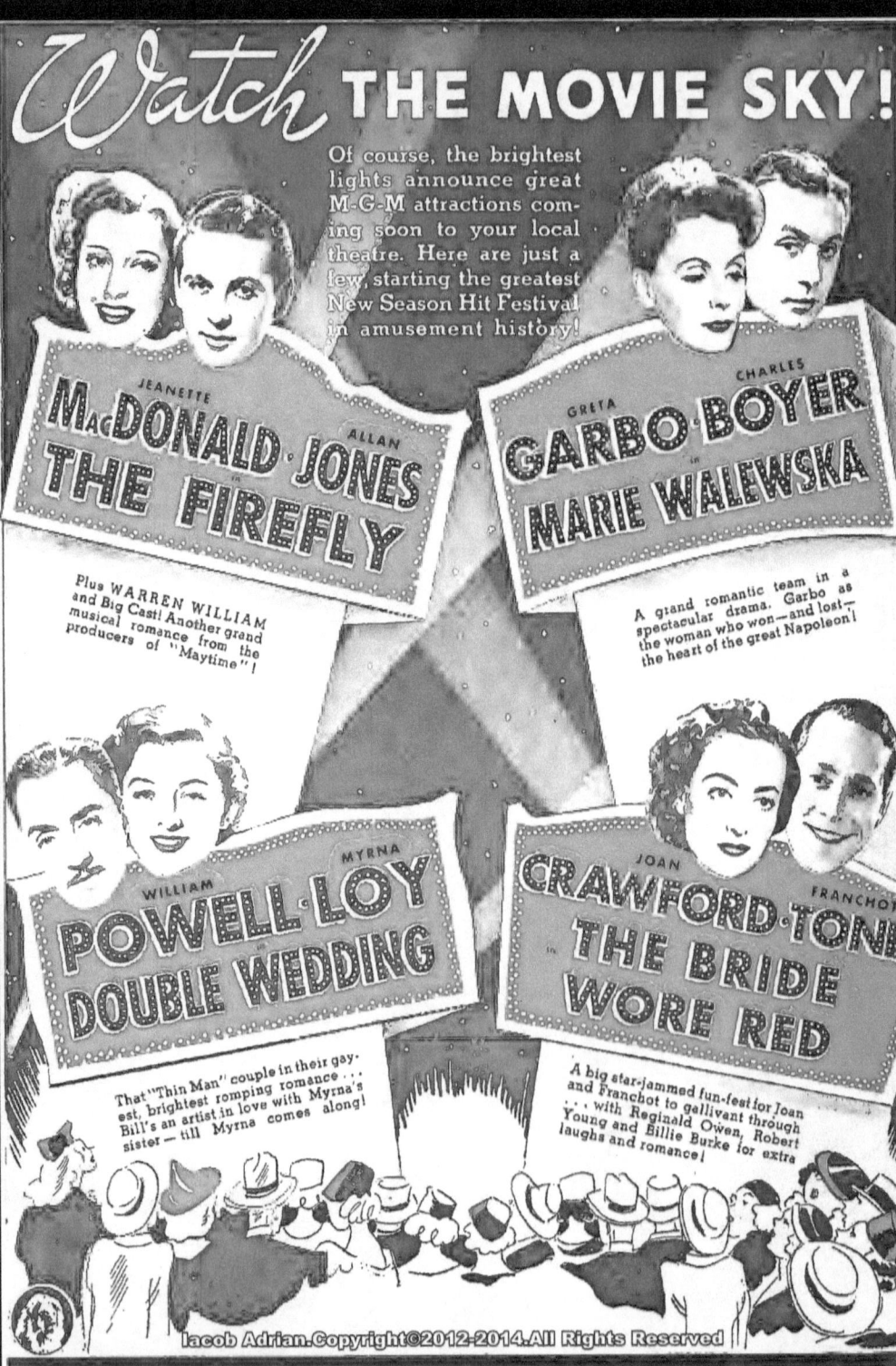

Watch THE MOVIE SKY!

Of course, the brightest lights announce great M-G-M attractions coming soon to your local theatre. Here are just a few, starting the greatest New Season Hit Festival in amusement history!

JEANETTE **MacDONALD** · ALLAN **JONES**
THE FIREFLY

GRETA **GARBO** · CHARLES **BOYER** in
MARIE WALEWSKA

Plus WARREN WILLIAM and Big Cast! Another grand musical romance from the producers of "Maytime"!

A grand romantic team in a spectacular drama. Garbo as the woman who won—and lost—the heart of the great Napoleon!

WILLIAM **POWELL** · MYRNA **LOY**
DOUBLE WEDDING

JOAN **CRAWFORD** · FRANCHOT **TONE**
THE BRIDE WORE RED

That "Thin Man" couple in their gay-est, brightest romping romance . . . Bill's an artist in love with Myrna's sister — till Myrna comes along!

A big star-jammed fun-fest for Joan and Franchot to gallivant through . . . with Reginald Owen, Robert Young and Billie Burke for extra laughs and romance!

METRO-GOLDWYN-MAYER'S GREATEST YEAR 1937-38

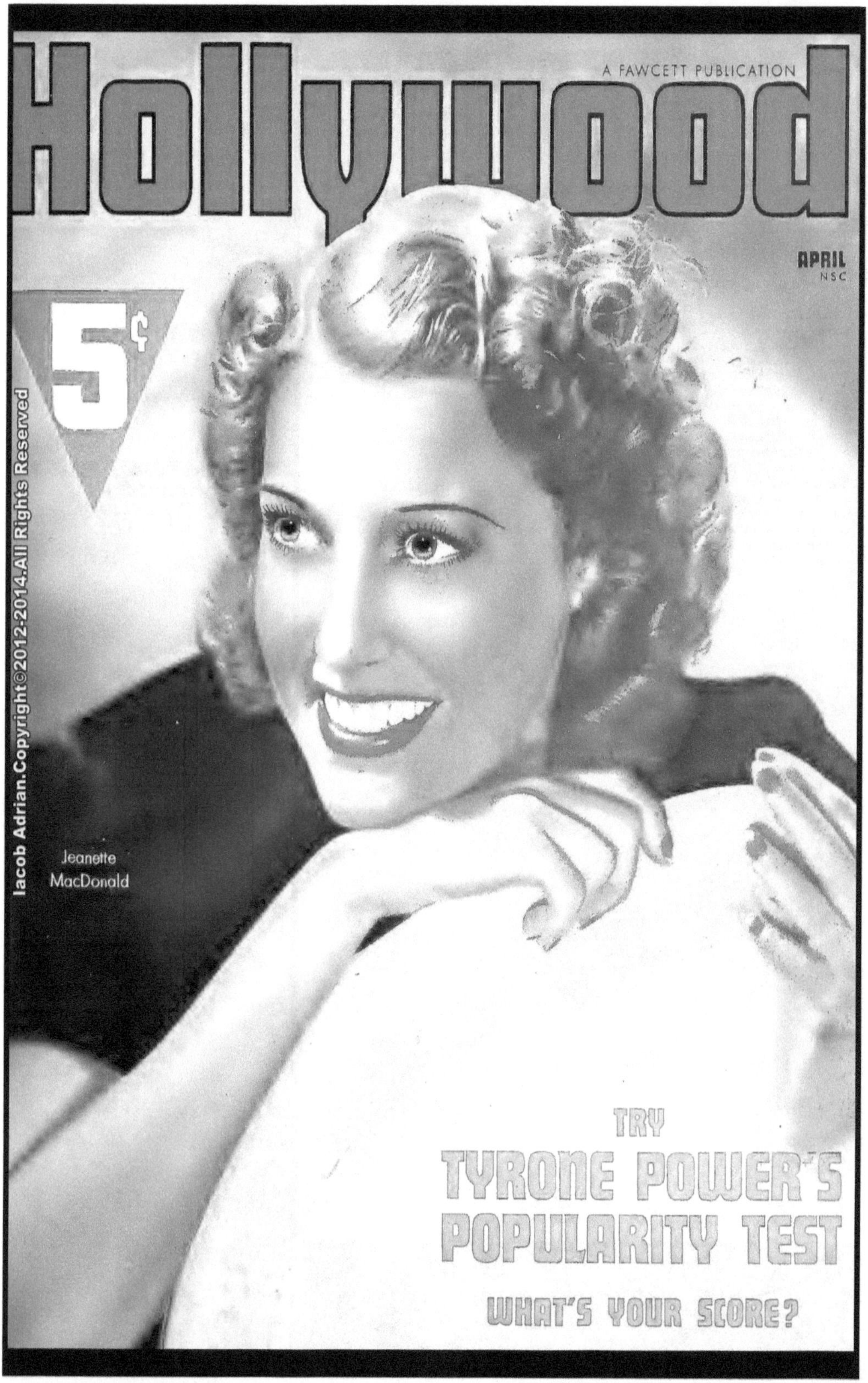

Hollywood

A FAWCETT PUBLICATION

APRIL
NSC

5¢

Jeanette
MacDonald

TRY
TYRONE POWER'S
POPULARITY TEST

WHAT'S YOUR SCORE?

WHEN A BRIDE HAS A CAREER

Even the busiest of stars must find time to give orders to the cook. Here is how one of them combines a career with the kitchen problems

By BETTY CROCKER

Jeanette MacDonald is one of the busiest girls in Hollywood, yet she must also run a kitchen and feed a hungry husband, just like many another bride.

How she does it and still manages to make hit pictures like *Girl of the Golden West*, sing on the radio, keep appointments with her voice teacher, and goodness knows how many other activities required of her, proves that even a career girl can have an efficient household if she puts her mind to it.

So for this month's culinary class, let's take up the cooking problems of the working wife and go into Mrs. Gene Raymond's kitchen for some ideas.

"When Gene and I married," Jeanette told me, "we knew that two careers in the same family would require careful planning at home. Every wife who carries on her own career, even if it takes only a few hours daily, knows that husbands must be fed and a house well managed if all is to be serene and happy.

"So the first thing we did was to go into the kitchen and list our cooking likes and dislikes. Fortunately, we both had similar tastes, as we discovered when we combined our lists as a guide for our cook. It's amazing how this guide has simplified matters so that the kitchen seems to run itself," with the minimum of attention from me."

Jeanette opened a kitchen cupboard. This was the guide, thumbtacked to the door:

BREAKFAST

Cereal. Fresh fruit (peaches, nectarines, figs, apricots) Stewed fruits. Baked apple. Hot milk, or weak tea.

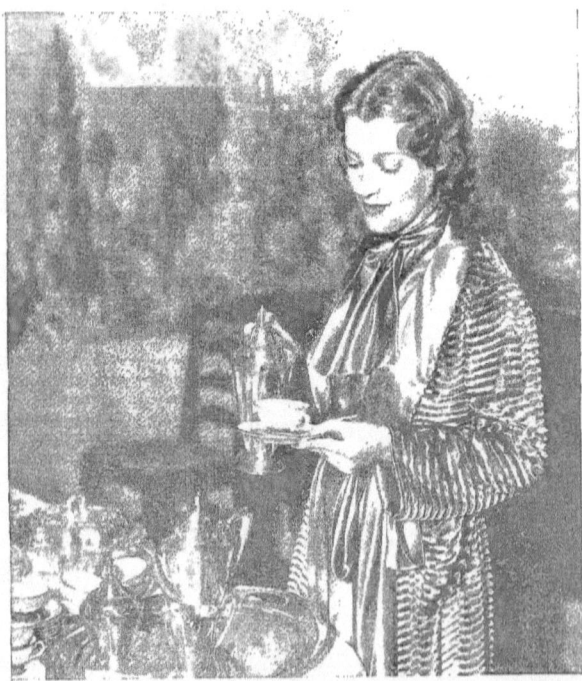

The coffee is always just right in the home of Jeanette MacDonald and Gene Raymond, and for the very good reason that she has learned how to combine two careers efficiently

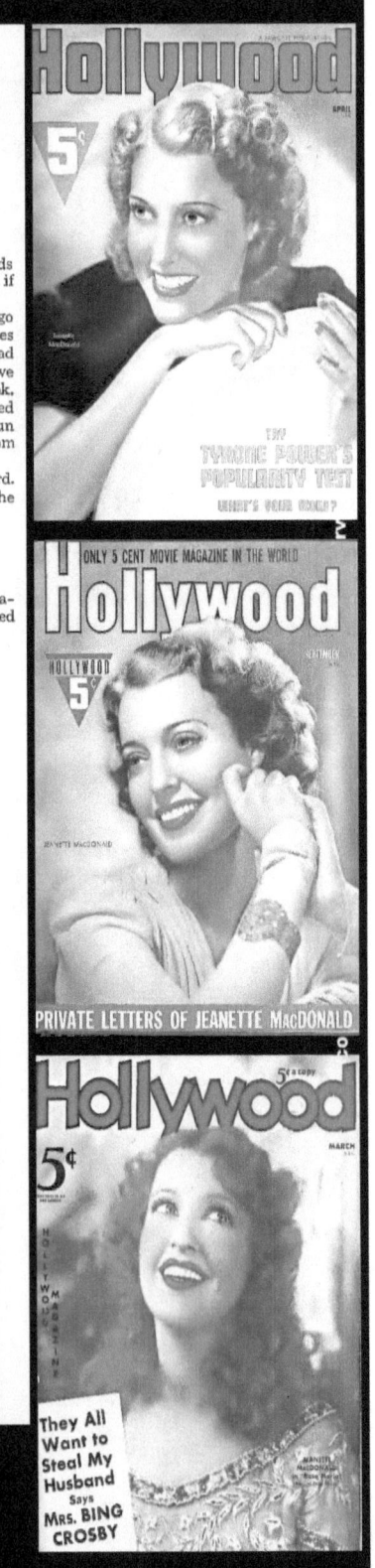

LUNCH

Potato Soup* or any home-made soup, using maggi sauce instead of meat, and including any assortment of vegetables. Green salad, French dressing. Hot rolls or bread if no potatoes on menu. Never meat for lunch.

DINNER

Meat: Any kind except pork or duck. Liver and sweetbreads* our favorite; next, tongue or grilled ground round steak.

Mushrooms: broiled in meat juice.

Eggplant: our favorite vegetable, prepared any way.

Other vegetables: carrots occasionally string beans, limas, green peas, baked squash. Never creamed vegetables. Always prepare Hollandaise sauce when serving broccoli.

Potatoes: b a k e d , mashed, creamed, steamed or buttered.

Desserts: Devils food cake* our special favorite.

Other desserts: Apple snow pudding, apple crisp, gelatine, baked apple, prune whip, fresh fruit tarts* .

*See recipes

"Why, every working wife ought to make a list of 'does and don'ts' like that," I exclaimed. "It should be easy to prepare meals with that guide.

"Exactly," smiled Jeanette. "When we're both in the midst of picture work, we practically live on soup. Cook dices a number of vegetables and lets the pot simmer all day. Potato soup, our favorite, is practically a meal in itself.

"Our favorite entree for dinner is a dish of sweetbreads, parboiled, on thick slices of ham. For dessert, we share a positive mania for devil's food cake. Fresh fruit tarts, you'll notice, are another favorite, or baked apples, cooked in sugar with flour and butter.

"And all are really easy to make if you follow a good kitchen tested recipe carefully."

Meanwhile, their affable cook, Margaret, was bringing out recipes from a neat card container for me to copy. Let's start with:

Potato Soup

2 cups milk
1 cup cooked potato
1 tbsp. grated carrot
1 tbsp. scraped onion
2 tbsp. butter
2 tbsp. all purpose flour
1 tsp. salt
Celery salt
Pepper

Method: 1. Heat milk in top of double boiler. 2. While milk is heating, rub cooked potato (either mashed or boiled) through a coarse sieve and measure. 3. Heat grated carrot and onion in the butter and blend in the flour. (Do not allow them to brown.) 4. Then stir into hot milk, and add potato, salt, pepper and celery salt. 5. Cook in double boiler 20 minutes, stirring occasionally. 6. Serve hot. AMOUNT: This makes 6 servings.

NOTE: You can use celery leaves in place of the celery salt if you have them, and then take them out before serving the soup. It's nice to add a little minced parsley as you serve the soup.

Fresh Fruit Tarts

Peel and stone 9 to 12 fresh apricots or 3 or 4 large peaches. Cut in slices and add sugar to sweeten (about ½ cup). Drip the juice from 1 orange over the apricots and sugar (about ⅓ cup orange juice) or drip the juice of a lemon over the peaches and sugar. Place in refrigerator to chill 2 or 3 hours. Brown on pan in oven 1 cup blanched whole almonds. Shave the toasted almonds in paper-thin strips. Take apricots or peaches from refrigerator. Drain and combine with the almonds. Pile into baked tart shells, and top each tart with a spoonful of sweetened whipped cream. A few of the almond slices may be reserved to garnish the top of the whipped cream.

Fresh Pineapple Tarts: To 1 cup fresh pineapple cut in small pieces, add enough granulated sugar to sweeten. Set in refrigerator to chill 2 or 3 hours. Drain juice from pineapple and fold it into sweetened whipped cream. (Use 1 cup whipping cream, then when it is whipped fold in 4 tbsp. confectioner's sugar.) Pile the pineapple-filled cream into tart shells and garnish each tart with a stoned fresh cherry. (The cherry can be filled with a nut.) Maraschino cherries can be used in place of fresh cherries.

Berry Tarts: Wash and hull 1 quart strawberries, raspberries, or blackberries and add enough sugar to sweeten. Pile sweetened berries immediately into baked tart shells. Garnish each tart with sweetened whipped cream and serve immediately.

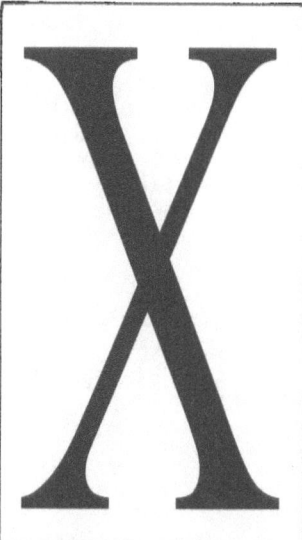

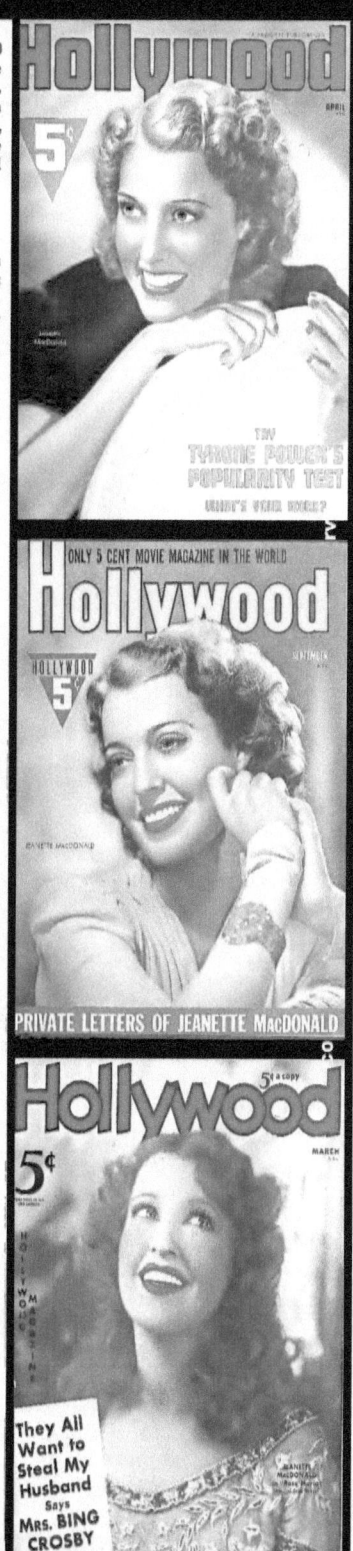

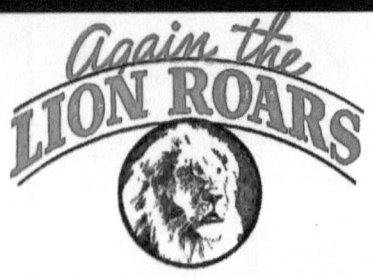

Again the
LION ROARS

METRO-GOLDWYN-MAYER PROUDLY PRESENTS THE SEASON'S GALA HIT!
EVERYBODY'S RAVING! EVERYBODY'S SINGING! EVERYBODY'S CHEERING!

Jeanette MacDONALD *Nelson* EDDY
in
SWEETHEARTS

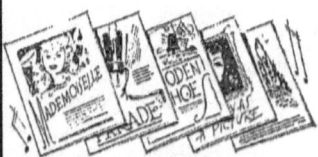

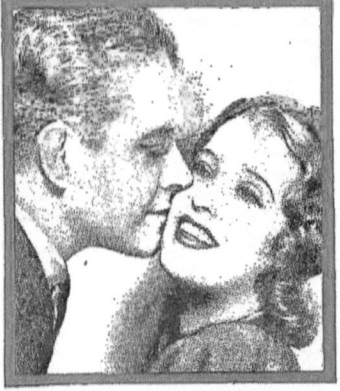

IT'S ENTIRELY IN BEAUTIFUL
TECHNICOLOR!

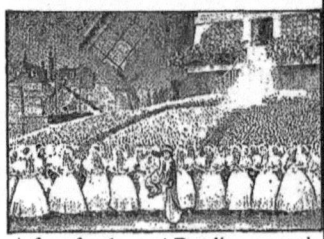

VICTOR HERBERT *Love-Songs!*
Thrilling melodies by the composer of "Naughty Marietta"! Hear your singing sweethearts blend their voices in *"Mademoiselle"*, *"On Parade"*, *"Wooden Shoes"*, *"Every Lover Must Meet His Fate"*, *"Summer Serenade"*, *"Pretty As A Picture"*, *"Sweethearts"*, . . . (Based on the operetta "Sweethearts", Book and Lyrics by Fred De Gresac, Harry B. Smith and Robt. B. Smith. Music by Victor Herbert)

A CAST OF FUNSTERS!

HEAVEN MADE THIS MATCH!
Their greatest musical romance! Thrilling as they were in "Rose Marie" and "May-time", you've never seen (or heard) Jeanette MacDonald and Nelson Eddy so pulse-quickening! Their love story will wring your heart! Their love-songs will charm you as never before! They're breath-taking in technicolor.

A feast for the eye! Dazzling spectacle becomes even more superb by the magic of Technicolor! Wait until you see the colorful "tulip scene" and other eye-filling spectacles!

A Metro-Goldwyn-Mayer Picture with
FRANK MORGAN
RAY BOLGER
FLORENCE RICE
MISCHA AUER
HERMAN BING
Douglas McPhail · Betty Jaynes
Reginald Gardiner · Gene Lockhart
Directed by W. S. VAN DYKE II · Produced by HUNT STROMBERG · Screen Play by Dorothy Parker and Alan Campbell

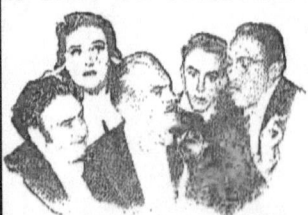

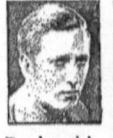 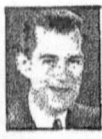

BRAINS
AT THE
HELM!

From left to right—garrulous Herman Bing, hilarious Frank Morgan, nimble-footed Ray Bolger, and Mischa Auer, that straight-faced, merry man . . . plus lovely Florence Rice in the background for extra romance!

Produced by Hunt Stromberg...Directed by W. S. Van Dyke II. They're still taking bows for "Marie Antoinette"—and who can forget their "Naughty Marietta" and all their other great hits!

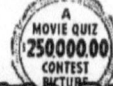
A MOVIE QUIZ
$250,000.00
CONTEST PICTURE

Beauty and the Blast

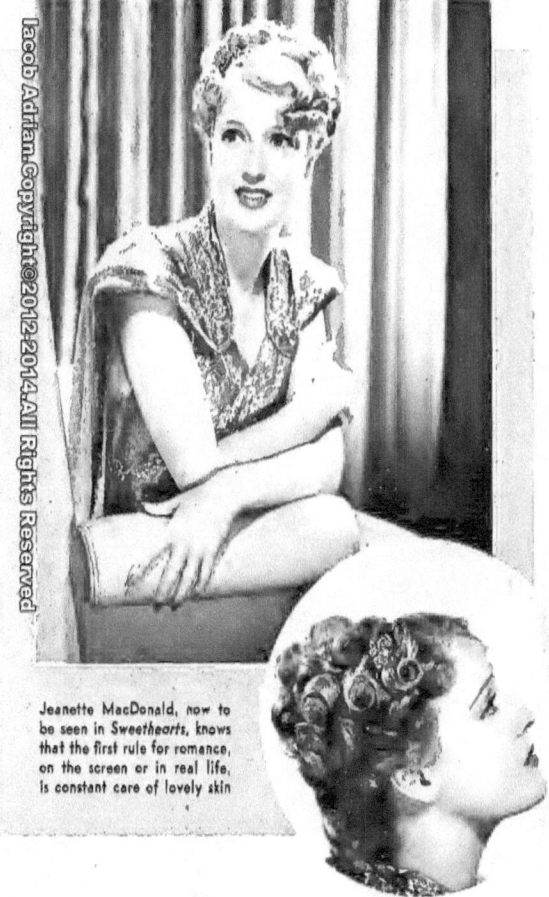

Jeanette MacDonald, now to be seen in *Sweethearts*, knows that the first rule for romance, on the screen or in real life, is constant care of lovely skin

No need for the wintry winds to be a menace to your beauty if you follow this good advice carefully

By ANN VERNON

■ Wintry blasts always pile my desk high with letters from readers, and most of the problems in them concern dry skin, chapped lips or red, raw hands. So I've decided to quote several typical winter-weather questions and give the answers. If you have another kind of problem, write to me, explaining your difficulty and I'll be glad to give it thought and send you a personal reply.

Q. *Although I use cold cream, my skin becomes very sensitive and dry in winter. It scales off in spots and I can't keep powder on. What to do?*

A. You must be omitting one of the "Big Four" rules of skin care—cleansing, lubrication, stimulation and protection. Or, at least, not being regular enough about practicing them. Your skin needs soap and water *and* creams. One of the reasons it is so touchy is that you don't stimulate the circulation enough, and a good scrubbing with soap (a mild one, of course) will whip up that lazy circulation. Try it at least once a day, and follow up with an application of lubricating cream. Leave a film of it on all night and it will banish that stiff, dry feeling as well as ugly scaliness. Always use a protective cream or lotion as a powder base. Powder alone rarely stays on over-dry skin; but you'll find that a good foundation will protect your skin from the chapping effects of wind and keep your powder intact.

If you "dries" don't believe my advice about soap, I wish you would write to me for the name of one that will convince you I'm right. It's a bland, milled soap, made with the finest oils. Its soothing but penetrating lather cleans without irritating and the price isn't irritating, either.

Ah! A dream of a foundation lotion to tell you about. No more scaly nose or fly-away powder for you now! It's a liquid emulsion, milky white and easy to spread over your skin. It clings to your skin and powder clings to it for hours. So endeth my praises—and your complaints.

Q. *Cold weather causes my lips to chap and crack painfully. I look awful with lipstick or without . . . How can I overcome this?*

A. The thin, sensitive skin of the lips usually needs babying. I'd advise you to apply lubricating oil or cream nightly, massaging it gently into the lips. And may I suggest a lipstick with a very creamy base that forms a protective film? It adapts itself to your own skin coloring, provides a rosy, blush tone—and its softening base keeps your lips as smooth and soft as velvet.

If you want an extra layer of protection and an extra layer of glossy allure, try a transparent film over your lipstick. All the stars use it to get that dewy, glistening look on their lips. Costs 50 cents and is made in Hollywood.

Q. *I'm so ashamed of my hands! They get terribly red and rough in cold weather although I'm only 21. Can you help me?*

A. There aren't as many oil glands in the skin on your hands as in other areas. That's one reason hands get rough and dry. The other reason is that they get more abuse. Women don't give them the care they lavish on their faces; and this in spite of the fact that hands have to do all the dirty work . . . So a hand beautifying routine should include constant use of lubricants to supply the natural oils that are missing or are removed by daily tasks. It should also place a ban on harsh, alkaline household soaps. You wouldn't wash your finest silk undies with cheap soap, so why treat your one and only pair of hands with less kindness?

I've been using a pale pink hand cream that I can't get along without in winter. Its fine oils vanish into the skin quickly (I am forever putting on and taking off my gloves, so I abhor any trace of stickiness!) and stay there, keeping my hands unusually soft and white. There's a jar of it on sale for a dime in ten cent stores. It contains enough to prove to you that the cream really spells hand beauty.

Please write me before February 15th if you wish the names of any of these products. Enclose a stamped, self-addressed envelope with 3 cents in U. S. postage.

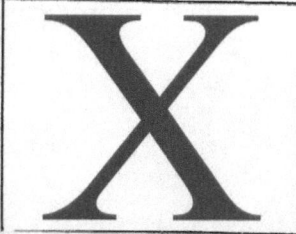

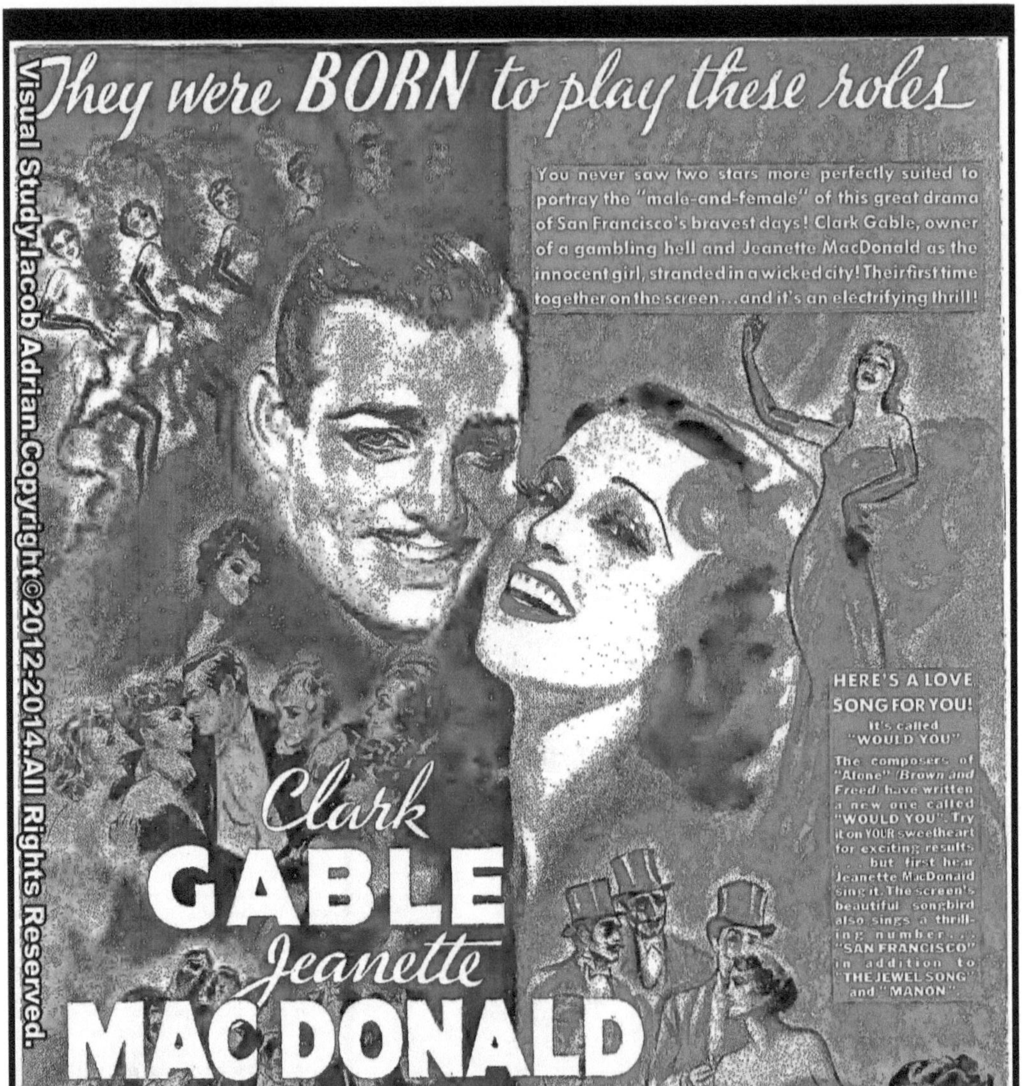

America's Songbird Chosen Queen of the Screen!

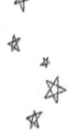

(22 Million Fans Voted Her FIRST in a Great National Newspaper Poll)

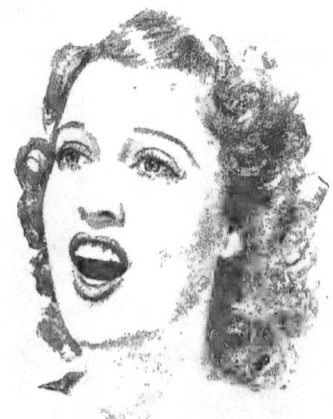

Jeanette MacDonald in "Broadway Serenade"

with L E W   A Y R E S · I A N   H U N T E R · F R A N K   M O R G A N

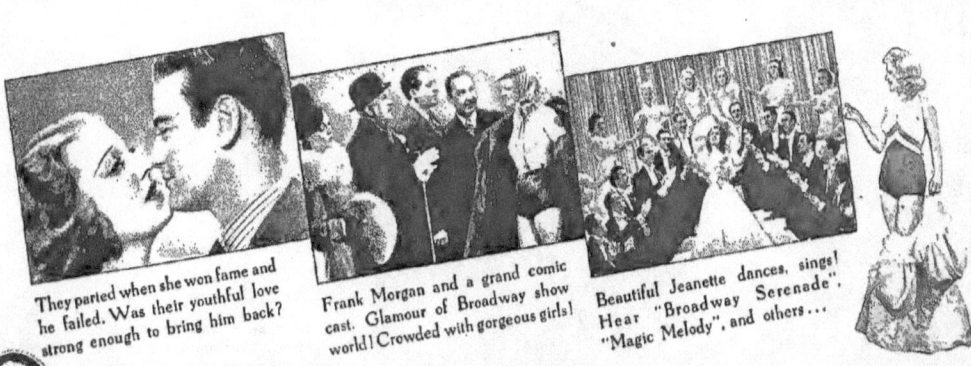

They parted when she won fame and he failed. Was their youthful love strong enough to bring him back?

Frank Morgan and a grand comic cast. Glamour of Broadway show world! Crowded with gorgeous girls!

Beautiful Jeanette dances, sings! Hear "Broadway Serenade", "Magic Melody", and others...

A ROBERT Z. LEONARD PRODUCTION · SCREENPLAY BY CHARLES LEDERER

Jeanette's Bright Ideas

Jeanette MacDonald would get along very nicely on her concert tour, were it not for the fact that her "bright ideas" do not always work

By LLEWELLYN MILLER

■ Traveling . . . for a movie star . . . is both pleasure and pain, especially if you are a movie star who always is getting bright ideas, like Jeanette MacDonald.

She came into her drawing room on the train bound for Philadelphia, helpless with laughter, fell into a seat and waved her hands in despairing indication that she had the giggles.

"He thinks I'm *crazy!*" she explained, none too clearly, and went off into another peal of laughter.

She did not look crazy. She looked very beautiful in a fragile wisp of a bluish-green wool dress, just the vivid color of her eyes. Slipping her arms out of her big mink coat, she

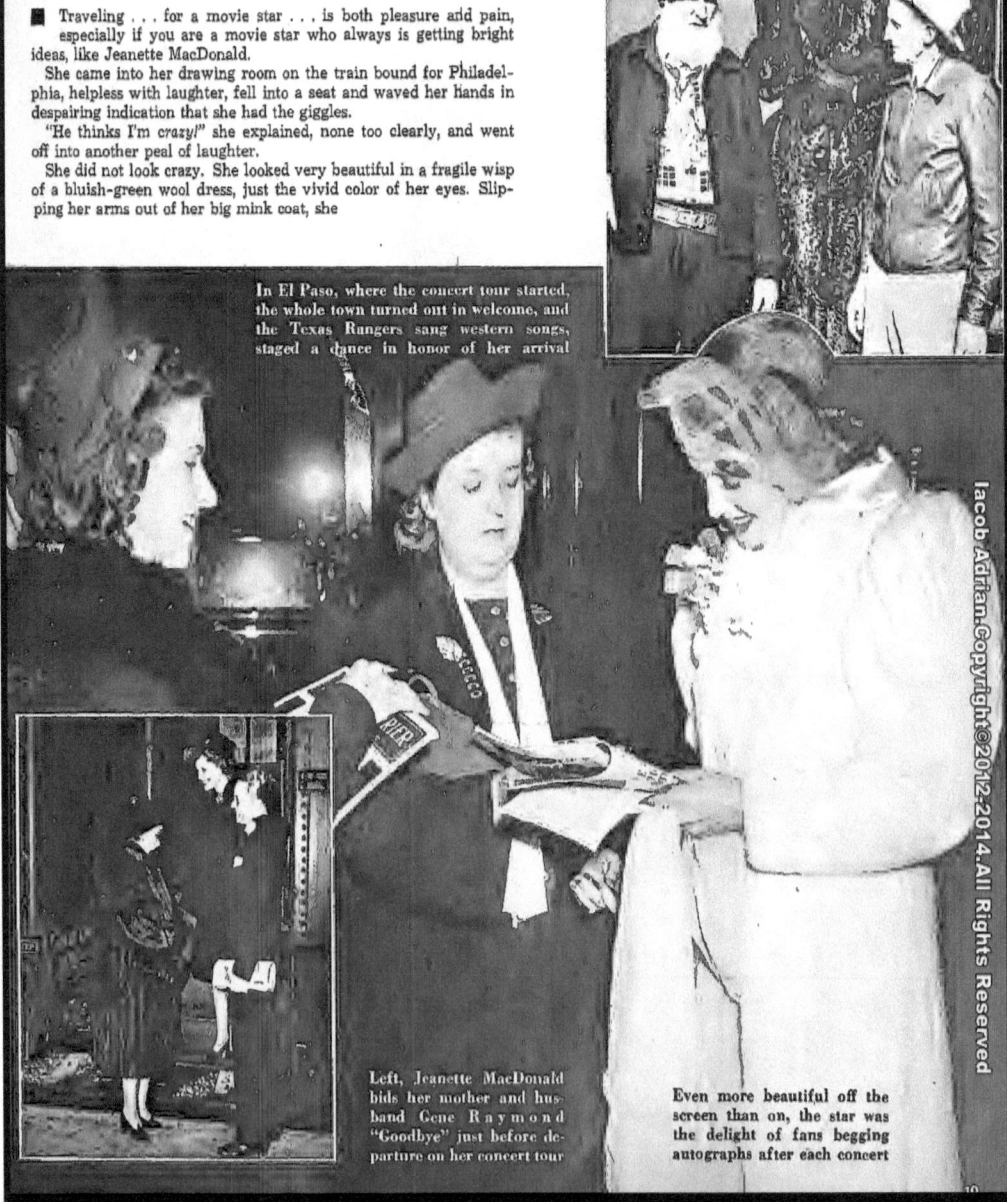

In El Paso, where the concert tour started, the whole town turned out in welcome, and the Texas Rangers sang western songs, staged a dance in honor of her arrival

Left, Jeanette MacDonald bids her mother and husband Gene Raymond "Goodbye" just before departure on her concert tour

Even more beautiful off the screen than on, the star was the delight of fans begging autographs after each concert

Jeanette's Bright Ideas

pointed one finger at it, and another at a rather indefinitely wrapped scarf that covered all but the very front of her red hair. The scarf *was* a somewhat foreign note in the striking ensemble . . . a bright blue and green silk bandanna more appropriate to motoring along California's beaches than to the smart avenues of New York or the crack flyer to Philadelphia.

"I'll *never* make him change his mind!" She shook with laughter, drew a deep breath, and turned sparkling eyes at the flat Jersey marshes that were whipping past the windows.

"It's all because everyone has been so wonderful on this tour," she explained. "Somebody is always doing something wonderful, or saying something nice, and I'm so used to saying 'Thank you' that a minute ago . . ." She collapsed into laughter again.

We were drawing into Elizabeth, New Jersey, before the whole story came out. On the same train was the whole Philadelphia Symphony Orchestra, returning from New York, and, as she made her way through the car, she stopped to greet one of the distinguished musicians.

"Ah," he said. "How are you?"

"And I said 'Thank you SO much!' No wonder he looked confused! Especially when he saw this." She pointed to the jaunty bandanna. "That's the result of one of my bright ideas."

Traveling with Miss MacDonald are her manager, the distinguished impresario, Charles Wagner; one of his associates, Edward Snowdon; her brilliant accompanist, Guiseppe Bamboschek; her own confidential secretary, Miss Sylvia Grogg, and her maid, but all of them combined have not been able to protect the star from some of her own bright ideas.

The bright idea that almost made her miss the train, turned a cab driver into a one-man streak of lightning, disrupted New York traffic, and surprised the Pennsylvania Station with her appearance in the gaudy bandanna was her latest. And it all came about because she had the bright idea of asking the editor of this magazine to ride down to Philadelphia with her to hear her concert in her own home town.

"We'll take an early train from Albany," she informed her company. "Then I'll have time to have my hair done in New York in peace and quiet with plenty of time to meet Llewellyn and catch the three o'clock train for Philadelphia."

There seemed to be nothing wrong with that plan. And that should have warned her traveling companions. There never is anything wrong with her bright ideas . . . at first. So, early in the morning, they arrived at the Albany depot to catch the train. But the train was late. Miss MacDonald had another bright idea. "We'll have breakfast while we're waiting," she suggested. That sounded all right, too, but they had not counted on the autograph hunters. A crowd gathered, and, while the coffee grew cold and the toast grew limp, Jeanette signed books and envelopes and menus with such charity that they almost missed the train when it finally did pull in.

"Oh, well, we'll have breakfast on the train," she comforted her hungry tribe as they walked away from the untouched food. But that was another bright idea that somehow didn't work. There was no dining car on that particular train! Late, very late, the star arrived at her favorite New York hairdresser's, and with a sigh of relief relaxed in the quiet little cubicle. It was warm under the drier, and the rush-

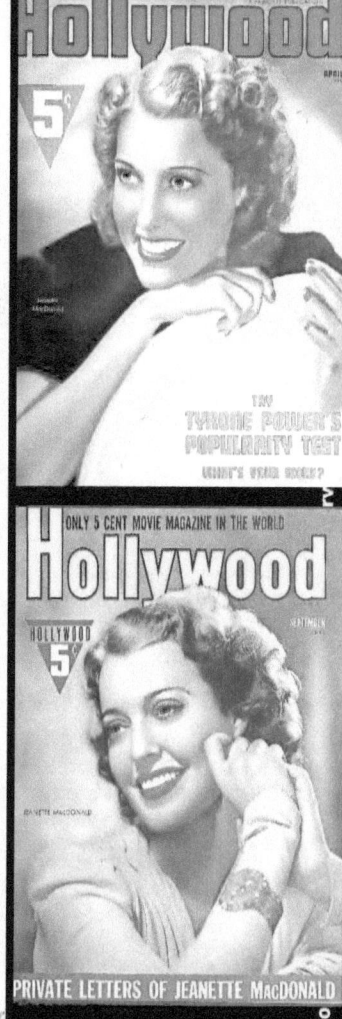

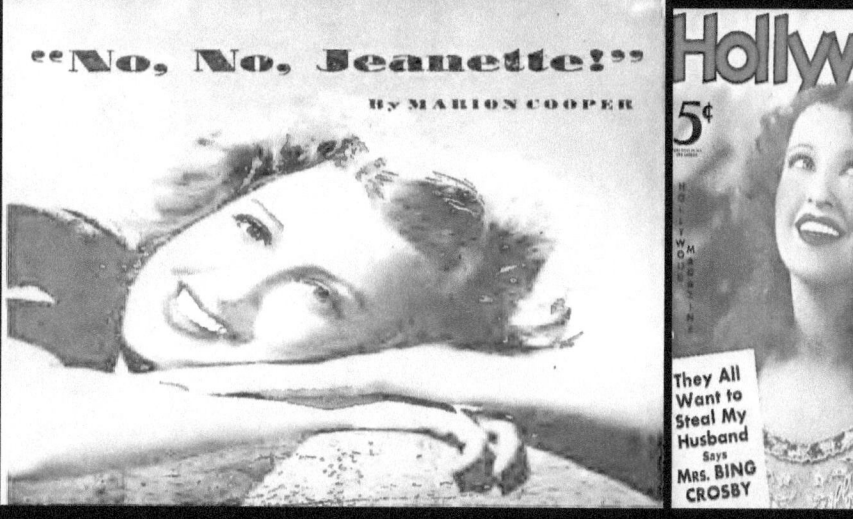

"No, No, Jeanette!"

By MARION COOPER

ing air had a soothing sound. The coffee had been hot and good. The shampoo had been fast and the curls had gone up perfectly. She closed her eyes, began to think happily of her concert in the famous old Academy of Music in Philadelphia where she had gone so many times when she was a little girl to hear the glamorous stars of the concert stage.

When she opened her eyes it was to give one shocked look at her watch, and start reaching for her possessions. There was no time to take out the pins. There was no time for the comb. There wasn't even time enough to catch the train, according to all usual standards of time and space.

Out of the beauty shop ran the distinguished star of screen and stage, winding the startling bandanna around her head. Up to the corner she hurried. Into a cab she popped.

"Pennsylvania Station," she said to the driver. "Do you think you can catch the three o'clock train?"

"Can't say," said the driver with that cool imperviousness to all human hopes and fears and aspirations except their own for which New York cabbies are justly noted.

"Double fare if you can!"

Something about her voice made him turn around for a good look. "Ain't you that movie star?" he asked. "Well, sure! Let's get going."

Without more ado, he swung into the middle of traffic, though the lights were against him.

"Beeeeeeeeeeeeep!" shrilled the traffic officer indignantly.

The cabbie slowed only slightly as he swung around on two wheels, gesturing back at Miss MacDonald with a wildly waving thumb. "Look who I got! It's Jeanette!" he roared. "She's gotta make a train! How about it?"

"For Jeanette, sure!" roared back the gallant officer. "Beeeeeeeeeeeeeep!" And he wheeled around, his white gloves gesturing back traffic in all directions, while her cab leaped across the intersection.

She closed her eyes. If there was going to be an accident, she didn't want to see it coming. She hoped that they would break the news gently to Gene. She hoped that her injuries would not be so severe that they could not move her to California. She hoped . . .

"Here you are!" cried the cabbie triumphantly. "All the time in the world to spare. You got three more minutes."

"For the widows and orphans' fund," she called back over her shoulder as she ran away from her change. "And thank you!"

"Wow! Thank *you*, Jeanette," he roared. "Come back soon!"

"So here I am," she finished. "And it was a bright idea, going down together, wasn't it? It's working out beautifully. Sometimes they do . . . though the one before the last was pretty bad . . ."

■ The bright idea before the last occurred to Miss MacDonald after she had spent a month on trains and in hotels. Under any circumstances, she has the greatest difficulty in getting enough sleep. The slightest noise keeps her awake. The most insignificant of sounds rouses her. In Hollywood, her habit is to snatch fifteen-minute naps all through the day in her studio dressing room whenever she is not needed on the set. But that plan is not very practical when on tour, and, by the time she reached the middle of her tour, she was desperately in need of several nights of sound, undisturbed slumber.

"I have a bright idea!" she announced. "Why don't we find out if there isn't a country club where we can stay instead of a hotel? Let's ask the manager."

The local concert manager was the soul of sympathy. There wasn't any country club open, but he thought he had the answer. A friend of his had a country place. Of course, it was closed for the winter, but it would be a simple matter to open it up. In fact, it was half opened already, in preparation for the spring. It was a little late to have dinner served there, but the house staff could be sent right out, beds would be ready, and certainly the place would be quiet . . . the nearest neighbor was three miles away.

It sounded like paradise to the star. After all, she had been traveling for five weeks, and, while the huge audiences that had turned out for her concerts were stimulating, the strain of performances and of

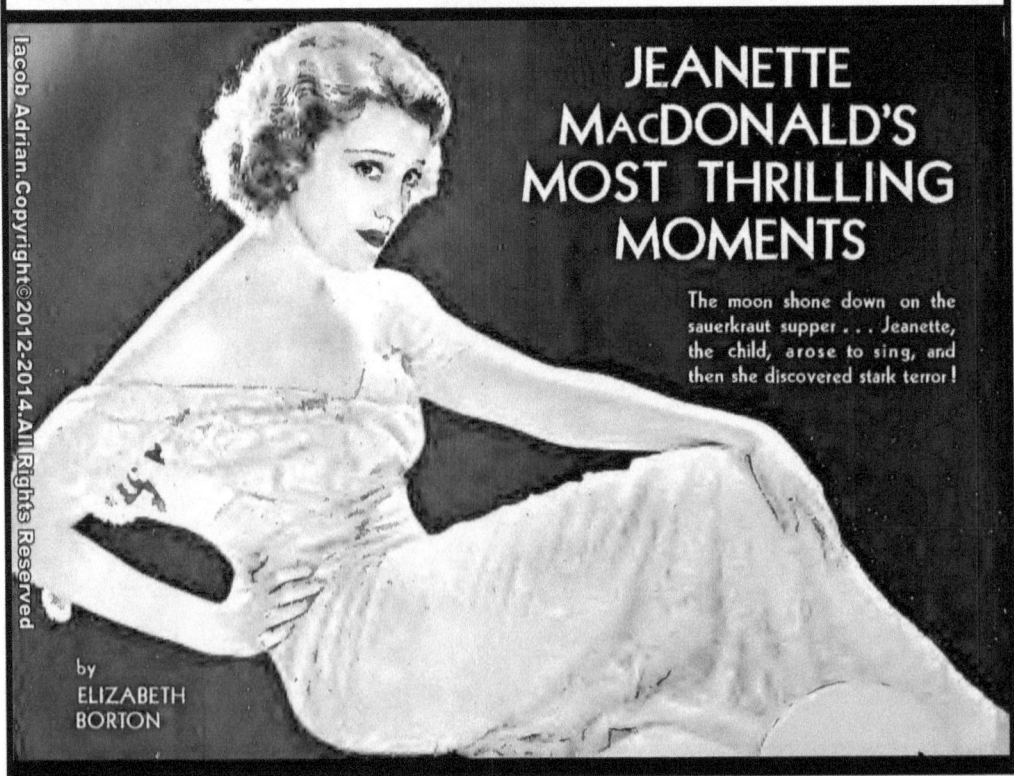

JEANETTE MacDONALD'S MOST THRILLING MOMENTS

The moon shone down on the sauerkraut supper . . . Jeanette, the child, arose to sing, and then she discovered stark terror!

by
ELIZABETH
BORTON

broken sleep in hotels was beginning to tell.

Leaving the men of her company looking rather envious, she set off gaily with Miss Grogg and her maid for the peace and quiet of the country.

"This was really a bright idea!" she said happily when they stepped into a charming living room after an hour's drive. A bright fire was crackling on the hearth, but otherwise the deep silence of the country was broken only by the cook's apology over dinner. There just had not been time, but she did hope that Miss MacDonald had found a nice place to dine on the way out.

The first blow came when they discovered that the nearest restaurant was forty-five minutes away. The second blow was the restaurant itself, which turned out to be one of the noisiest road houses in the whole South. The third blow came after the servants had departed for the night, and Miss MacDonald lay down gratefully in the peace and quiet of her country bedroom.

"Glug!" said the radiator. "Glug. Glug, Crack, glug. Crack-glug-crack-glug-glug-glug-crack-crack." The uproar grew in volume, building from wheezy gasps to the rousing complaint of a Model T Ford protesting at a hill, while three completely wide-awake young women ran around all over the house, turning off radiators like mad. They turned off everything they could find, but still the uproar went on.

Then they got the fourth blow. The telephone was not connected, and the nearest neighbor was three miles away in some unknown direction!

The fifth blow came when, hours later, they pulled up in front of the hotel, only to discover that it was also housing a convention . . . a convention that was having a lovely time, and gave every sign of continuing its celebration all night . . . a convention that promptly voted Miss MacDonald its favorite star, and honored her with a serenade!

It was a beautiful compliment, but not what might be considered restful. At that, Miss MacDonald added ruefully, it was quieter than the country.

Of such things is the painful side of traveling for a movie star who likes her sleep. On the brighter side of the picture are the enormous audiences that have packed concert halls all the way across the country, the enthusiastic response to her favorite song, "Let Me Always Sing," which Gene Raymond wrote, the plans for her appearance in grand opera which are beginning to take shape in the minds of more than one person who has heard her sing in concert. Studio duties demand a goodly portion of her time, but under any circumstances, she will repeat her concert tour next year. "I really think it's a bright idea, don't you?" she asked.

Her whole company jumped at the words, then they relaxed. After all, *some* of her bright ideas do work out, and there could be no doubt that a repeat tour was an idea that could not be anything but a shining success.

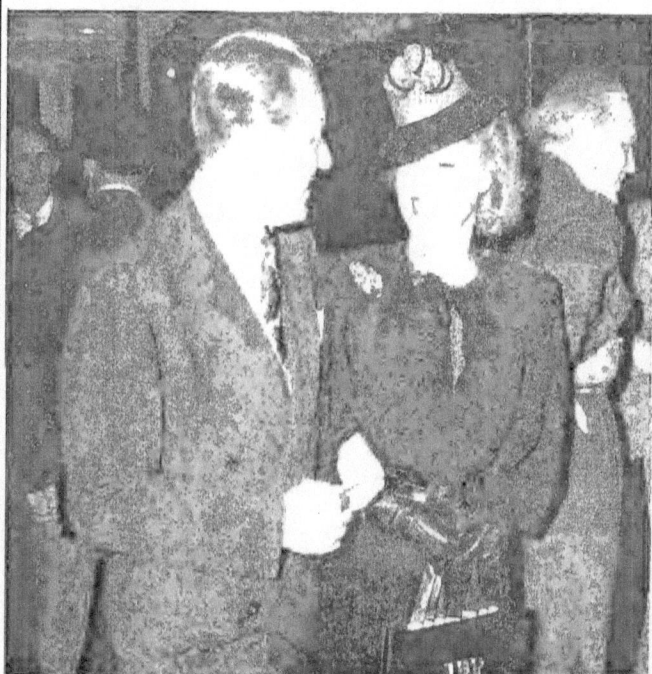

Fawcett photo by Rhodes

Gene Raymond and Jeanette MacDonald, snapped leaving a preview, seem delighted about something. Maybe it is the striking portrait of Jeanette that you will see on next month's HOLLYWOOD Magazine. Gene is now making *Highway to Romance* at RKO-Radio, and Jeanette will be seen soon in *New Moon* opposite Nelson Eddy

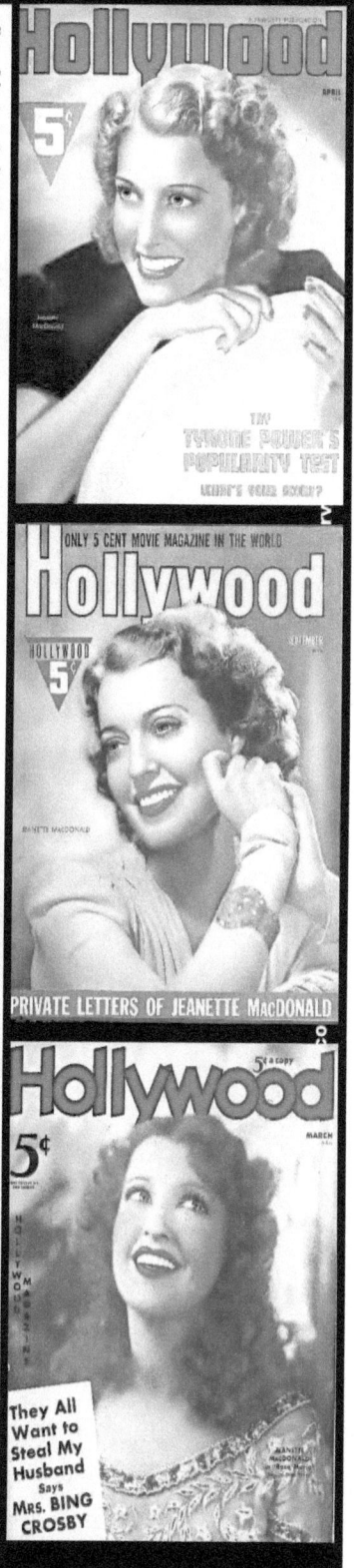

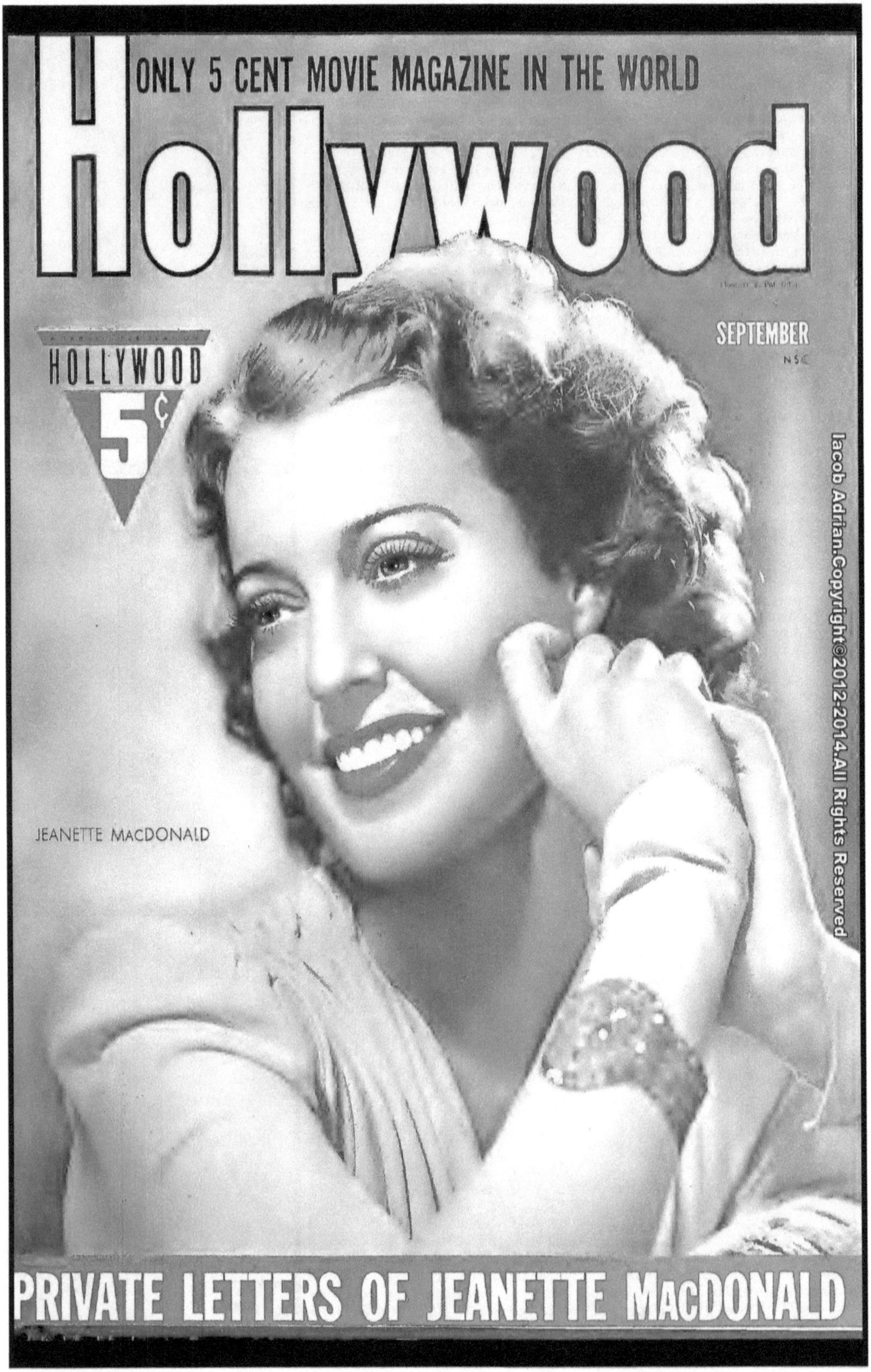

ONLY 5 CENT MOVIE MAGAZINE IN THE WORLD

Hollywood

HOLLYWOOD
5¢

SEPTEMBER

NSC

JEANETTE MacDONALD

PRIVATE LETTERS OF JEANETTE MacDONALD

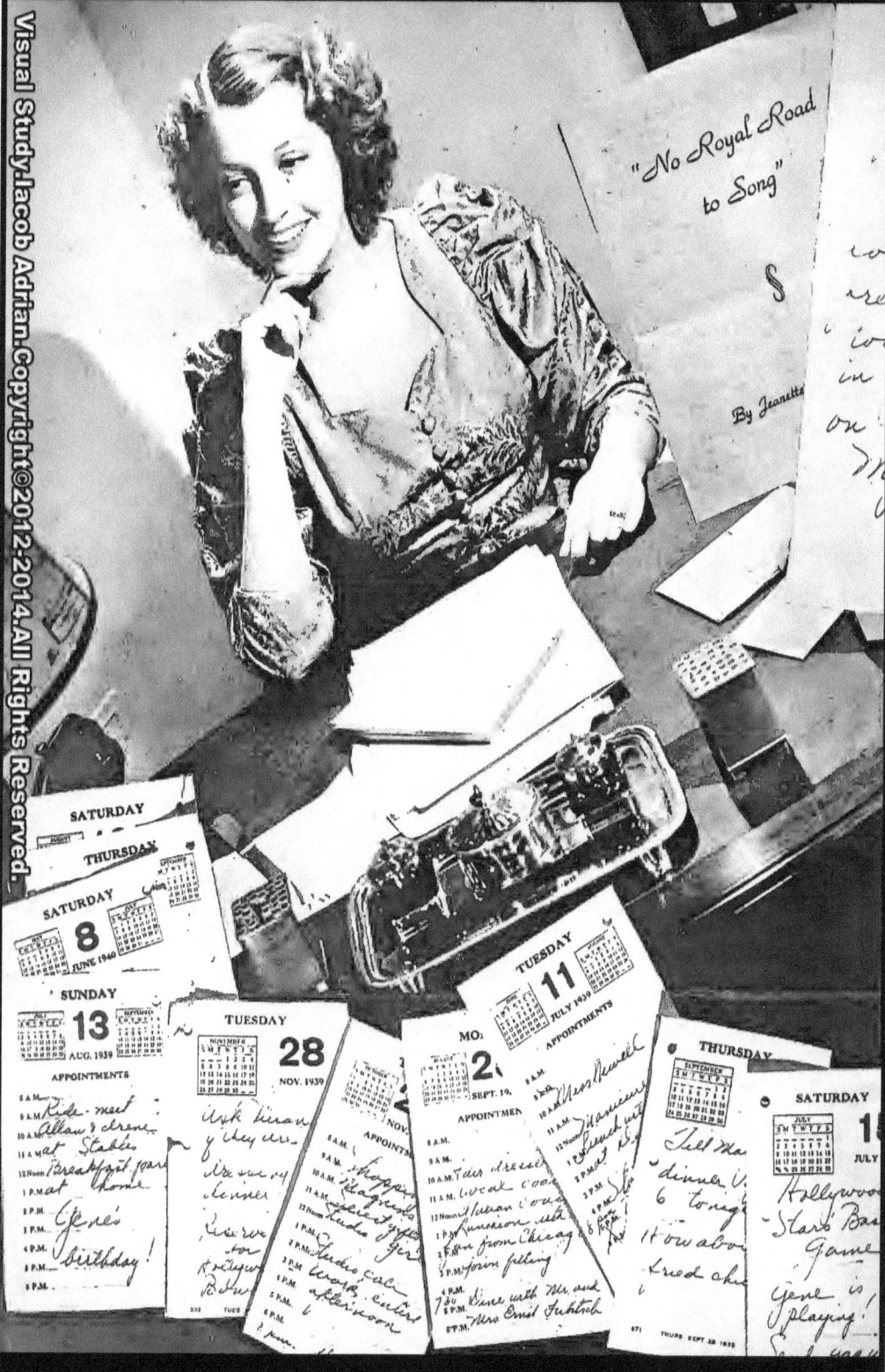

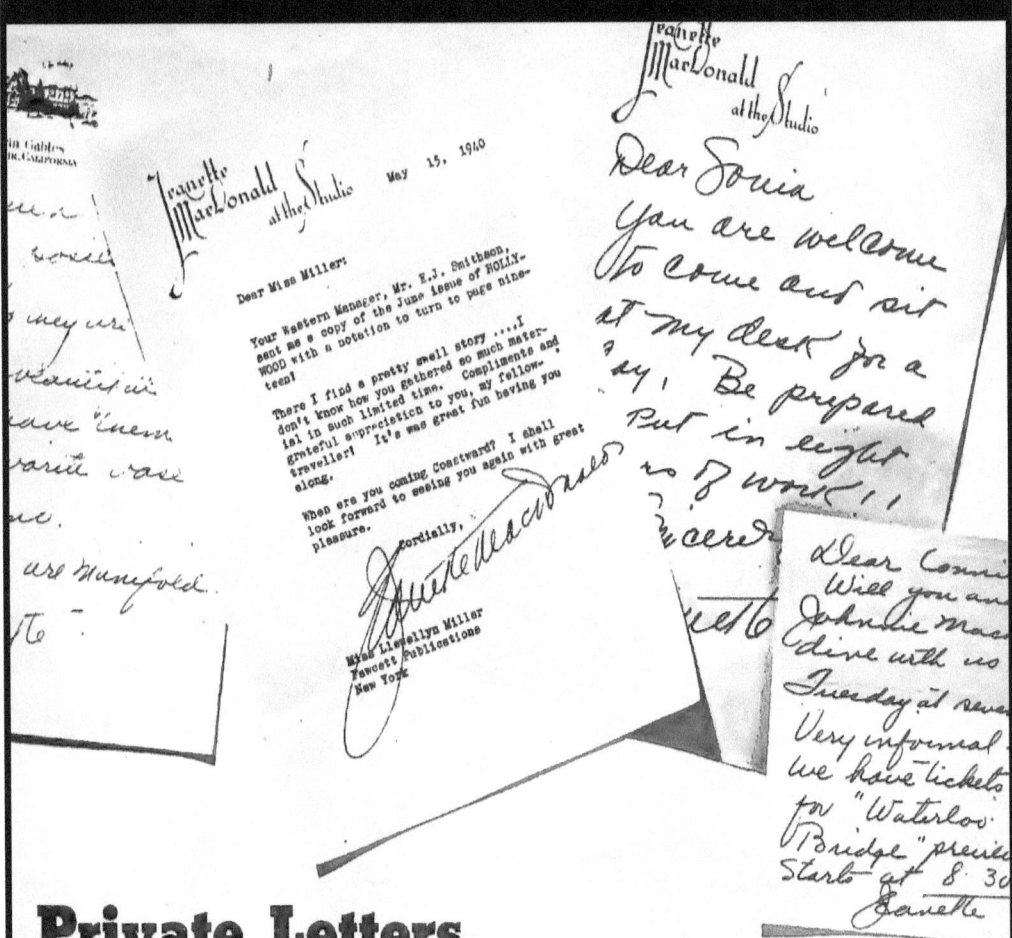

Private Letters
of Jeanette MacDonald

Jeanette MacDonald is a living proof of the saying, "The more you have to do, the more you can accomplish."

Even in the midst of picture production, when there seem to be a dozen different demands on every minute of the day, her desk remains reasonably clear, her correspondence is never neglected, even though her letters frequently number hundreds a week. Jeanette is an inveterate letter writer because she is a firm believer in putting things on paper. Once in a while things "carried in the head" are forgotten and produce hurt feelings or embarrassments, so a flurry of little notes about dozens of different matters leaves her studio dressing-room every day. Her calendar pad is crowded with jotted notes of reminders to herself and her secretary.

When she is busy at the studio, letters are dictated on the set between scenes,

The correspondence of a movie star covers dozens of different matters. Here is your chance to spend a day at Jeanette's desk and see how she deals with this important problem

By SONIA LEE

in her own quarters at noontime, and at any other moment she may find herself free. When she has the day at home, part of each morning, frequently a good part of the whole day, is spent at the dainty writing table in her sitting room.

The first half hour always is devoted to letters to intimate friends . . . bread-and-butter notes, acceptances of invitations, thank-you notes and her own invitations. These she usually writes on double cards, the size of a calling card. "Mr. and Mrs. Gene Raymond" is engraved on the front, and her note, in long hand, of course, is jotted on the inside.

Notes to her associates at the studio regarding matters incident to work are dictated to her secretary who later types them.

Today there is a matter of wardrobe. Adrian had submitted s k e t c h e s and samples. Jeanette writes:

"Dear Adrian: The sketches are divine! And I agree with you on the coloring. The blue bodice should be a trifle deeper than the skirt, blending the two

Private Letters of Jeanette MacDonald

shades of blue at the waistline. "The sample of the gray tulle is lovely. When will you need me for a fitting? Will Wednesday be convenient for you?" She signs it—"Sincerely, Jeanette"—the signature which goes on all her letters to co-workers at the studio, from executive to wardrobe girl.

The greatest letter-writing chore Jeanette MacDonald has is answering the numerous fan letters which come to her desk for personal attention and reply. These are letters segregated from the thousand she receives each week, by her secretaries. They include letters from fan correspondents of long standing; letters which definitely ask advice on a personal or a career problem; letters which ask for the intangible gift of courage.

If Jeanette is working, she reads these letters between scenes, makes memos in pencil which are the basis of a reply by her secretary, or later on for her dictated answer. Frequently, when there is long leisure between scenes, she dictates on the set.

On this day, as we sit at Jeanette's desk —a small battalion of human problems faces her.

There is the letter from Arva: "Dear Jeanette," she writes, "I'm twelve years old. At eleven my voice matured, but now something's happened. I can't hit those high notes at all. I'm sort of hoarse or something. Is my voice gone? Were you that way? Is there anything I can do? Anything I can gargle? I'm almost desperate . . . please help me. My voice is my whole life."

Jeanette makes a note on the back of the letter. She writes: "Answer this kid and tell her I lost my voice around the same age and had to stop singing for a year and a half. Tell her that frequently happens. By continuing to sing she may ruin her voice. She'll just have to be patient and trusting. Meanwhile she can study French and Italian."

From Helen: "I'm studying voice seriously, but I'm having teacher trouble. I have recently changed teachers and find myself singing flat and straining a great deal. You sing so easily. What should I do?"

Jeanette quiets Helen's fears. "All singers hit occasional snags. Don't try to rush," she writes.

Enclosed with this reply will be a little leaflet entitled, "No Royal Road to Song," which was written by Jeanette to serve more or less as a standard reply to aspiring young singers. It answers many of the usual questions asked her.

These young singers write her not only regarding training and the problems of a singer, but frequently ask advice on debut programs.

Recently a young singer was to have her first radio audition.

"What should I sing—an operatic aria? It is for a children's program."

"No," Jeanette had replied, "sing something simple—perhaps an American folk-song. A Stephen Collins Foster ballad would be advisable."

Today there is a letter from the young aspirant, telling Jeanette of success and a radio contract.

Jeanette has close contact with the fans who have written her for years. In their letters they tell her much of their intimate lives, advise her of important events and the important things which have happened to them.

This morning there is such a note from Ethel. "I had hoped to have a daughter to name for the two women I admire most —my mother and you," she writes. "But it was a boy, so I named him for the person you love best—Gene. He's a handsome baby, perfect in every way. He weighed eight pounds, one ounce at birth. He has curly blond hair and blue eyes."

Jeanette sends thanks and congratulations—and in a day or so a small gift will go to Gene's namesake. (Jeanette makes a note on her pad.)

From England Clarice writes: "There is a war now, but I saw one of your pictures last night. You don't know what it did for me. It was like a tonic—a visit to another, happier world . . . a letter from you would mean so much. Would you write?"

From an ambulance driver in England— a girl who has written to Miss MacDonald for years, there is also a letter. "I'm so glad you were pleased with the little present. I have been on duty for forty-eight hours without a break . . . we are all tense, but calm and ready for any emergency . . . if anything happens to me, I want you to know how much all your kindnesses have meant to me." There is no return address. Jeanette's lips are held steady by effort as she finishes reading.

From a very old lady, eighty-four, there is a brief letter. "Thank you for the kind of pictures you make. There is tenderness in all the love scenes you play. I think that you make young people, no matter how modern and sophisticated they may be, feel that true and sincere love is the finest thing in life after all, and you help old people re-live their lost youth once again."

"Letters such as these," Jeanette comments, "make an actress feel her responsibility." She thanks her correspondent for her gratifying letter.

From fourteen-year-old Marie there is a letter:

"My father wrote you while I was in the hospital and you sent me a picture of yourself and wrote on it, 'Get well in a hurry', and signed your name. I was in an awful accident and came out of it with only one arm. I've been singing since I was a baby and ever since I can remember I went to see your pictures and tried to sing like you do. Do you think I can be happy without an arm?"

"A lot of famous people have been physically handicapped," Jeanette writes. (Aside to her secretary: "Find something about the life of Helen Keller and send it to Marie.")

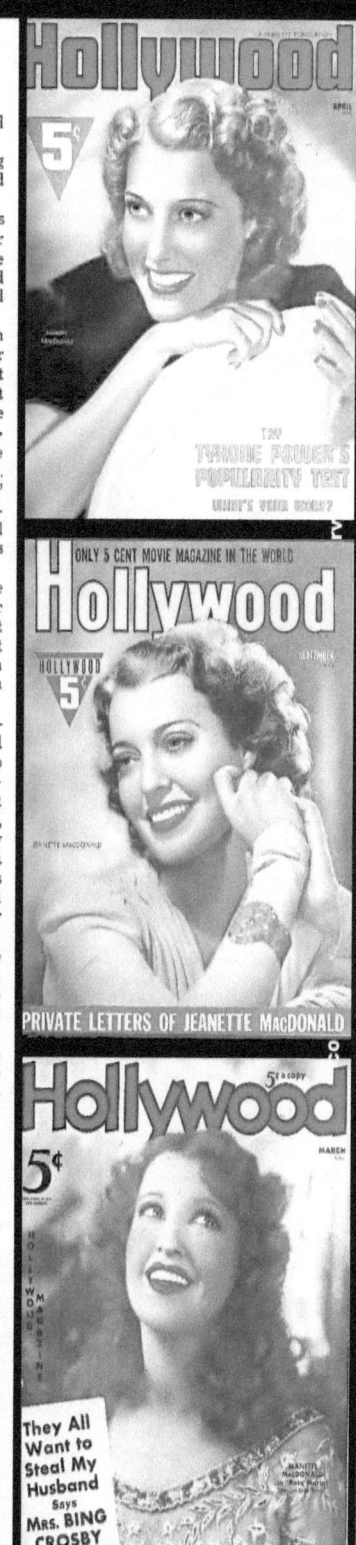

PRIVATE LETTERS OF JEANETTE MacDONALD

They All Want to Steal My Husband Says MRS. BING CROSBY

Among Jeanette's regular correspondents is a bed-ridden old lady. To Jeanette come pages of the philosophy she has acquired in the many years of enforced inactivity. She is a gentle and a patient person. While she has only seen one of Jeanette's pictures, her music library contains all the records the star has made.

Today's letter says: "I always feel so grand when I receive a letter from you. I hold it and think about it before opening it. If I could only hear you speak—just once."

(Jeanette to her secretary: "Let's telephone her long-distance next Sunday afternoon.")

A young girl writes: "Since 1931 you have been my firm friend . . . You were responsible for my scholastic triumphs, and often the thought of you saved me from slacking. I always did my very best for you. Every time I made a grade, I felt you were proud of me, and when I failed you did your best to sympathize. It was your inspiration which has prompted me to success . . . I have just won a musical scholarship . . ."

"Your success has made me very happy," Jeanette replies. "And I'm humbly grateful for the part you feel I've played in it."

A mother wrote some months ago: "My little girl is a cripple . . . completely helpless . . . she has been talking about your scheduled concert in our city, and is heartbroken because she can't go. But she tires so quickly . . . I'd give anything in the world if we could bring her to your concert, but the doctor forbids it. I know this is presumptuous . . . but would you say 'hello' to her, if we brought her to see you at your hotel? . . . her pleasures are so limited."

Jeanette had invited the child for tea. There was more than tea and Jeanette's presence waiting for Rhona when she had arrived—telegrams from Hollywood celebrities.

And the letter now on Jeanette's desk is the aftermath. "Rhona started mending from that day on . . . we pray for you every night."

From the time Gertrude A.'s children were in pinafores, she has written to Jeanette MacDonald her hopes and her ambitions for her two small daughters. Later, when neither one actively displayed the musical talent which the mother fondly suspected at first, she brought her disappointment to the singing star. "I had hoped," she wrote, "that they would realize the ambitions I, myself, always had, but wasn't able to do anything about . . . I feel so let down."

"Isn't there a youngster in your community with real talent who needs a little help? Why don't you interest yourself in the welfare of such a child? . . . It will give you immeasurable personal satisfaction . . ." Jeanette had written.

Gertrude A. did find a worthy, ambitious, talented girl and transferred her interest in music to her. She arranged for scholarships. She encouraged and helped financially. Through all this process of selection and progress, Gertrude A. reported regularly to Jeanette. When the girl won her first scholarship. When she

had her first audition. When she made her concert debut.

"Marcia has a radio contract," Gertrude A.'s letter tells Jeanette this morning. "She owes it all to you."

"Not to me," Jeanette replies. "But to you who stood at her side all these years."

Jeanette frequently finds herself in the role of a guide to young girls.

This letter from Celeste, is an example: "Boys are attracted to me, but I cannot keep them as friends . . . When they find I have high ideals and won't pet, they drop me. I met a boy . . . I liked him . . . but he doesn't call me up any more . . . his grievance was that Mama made him bring me home at twelve. I've lost faith in men . . . It seems as if the modern generation has a scheme which I cannot fit."

Jeanette replies: "Don't lose faith. The things your parents have taught you are wise. As you get older you'll know it to be true. You'll find happiness . . . but be willing to wait for it."

Give me courage . . . give me hope . . . give me strength . . . give me faith . . . this is a never-ending refrain in the letters from the weak and the meek and the sick.

There is a little girl in a hospital near New York City. A picture of Jeanette MacDonald is on her bedside table. Periodically a new one arrives—one in the costume of her latest picture.

Months ago her guardian had written to Jeanette: "You are one person who has been the inspiration for all her courage . . . You have created in her the desire to walk and to dance, the one thing which has been declared impossible for her by all the doctors who ever examined her. But the miracle is happening . . . she is sitting up alone . . . she says she is going to walk soon . . . She keeps a scrap book about . . . she has read over and over again the story about the time when you were advised to forget your desire to sing, how you refused to give up. This has inspired her to accomplish the seemingly impossible."

And another letter about this child: "She is a lonely little soul . . . She has been cast aside by her parents because of her handicap, and you have helped fill that breach . . . When other children talk about home and parents she says she thinks of you and pretends that she has some one also who really cares for her . . . Often when I come home, I find she has her many scrap books about you spread out on her bed, your pictures and letters standing up around her, and she is living in a little make-believe world of her own . . ."

Letters from Jeanette arrive for this little girl with regularity. When steel braces are to be fitted, when painful treatments are in progress, the letters are timed to arrive at the psychological moment. "I'll be expecting to see you when I come East . . . You'll surely be walking by then," the letters will repeat.

For almost three years now, Jeanette has been writing this invalid. For three years she has been pouring courage into a child.

Today Jeanette writes an answer to a report of definite progress: "Hooray—for those first steps. I knew you could do it."

No wonder Jeanette MacDonald takes a day at her desk seriously!

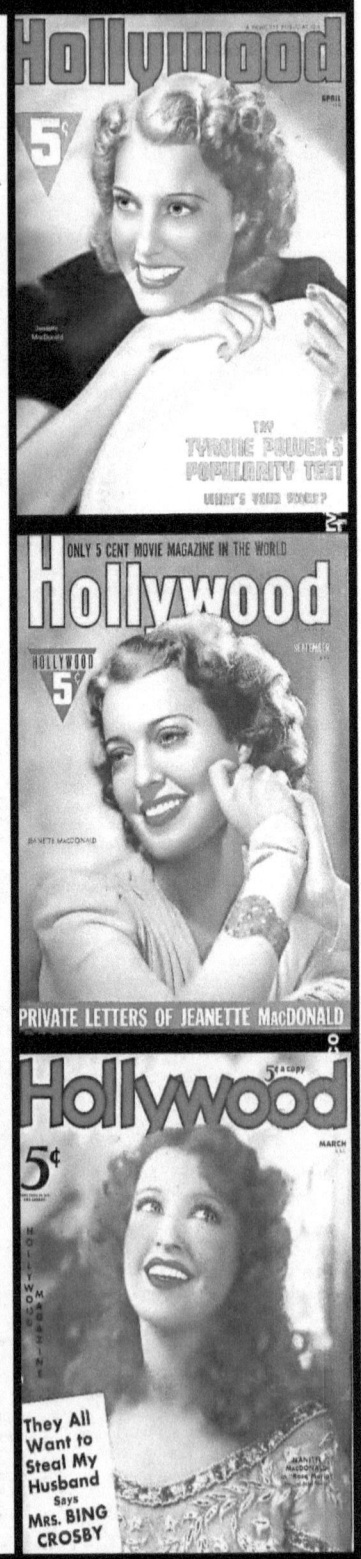

Sweethearts

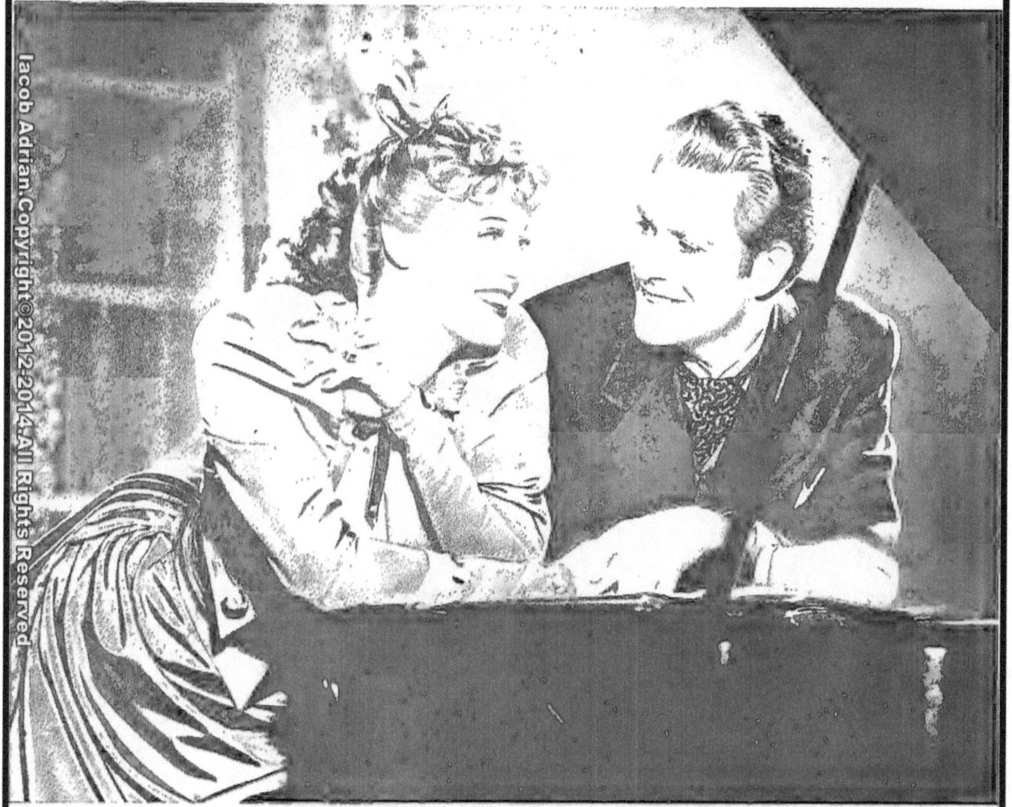

Of all the musical thrills your singing sweethearts ever gave you, here is the greatest! Ziegfeld's memorable stage triumph—crowded with romance and melody—becomes in glorious Technicolor a picture you'll never forget. Metro-Goldwyn-Mayer proudly presents...

JEANETTE   NELSON
MacDONALD · EDDY
in NOEL COWARD'S

Bitter Sweet

Photographed in Technicolor with
GEORGE SANDERS, IAN HUNTER, FELIX BRESSART
Original Play, Music and Lyrics by Noel Coward. Screen Play by Lesser Samuels
Directed by W. S. VAN DYKE II. Produced by Victor Saville
A METRO-GOLDWYN-MAYER PICTURE

Songs: "THE CALL OF LIFE" "I'LL SEE YOU AGAIN" "WHAT'S LOVE" "TOKAY" "DEAR LITTLE CAFE" "LADIES OF THE TOWN" "ZIGEUNER"

Looking In On
Jeanette and Gene

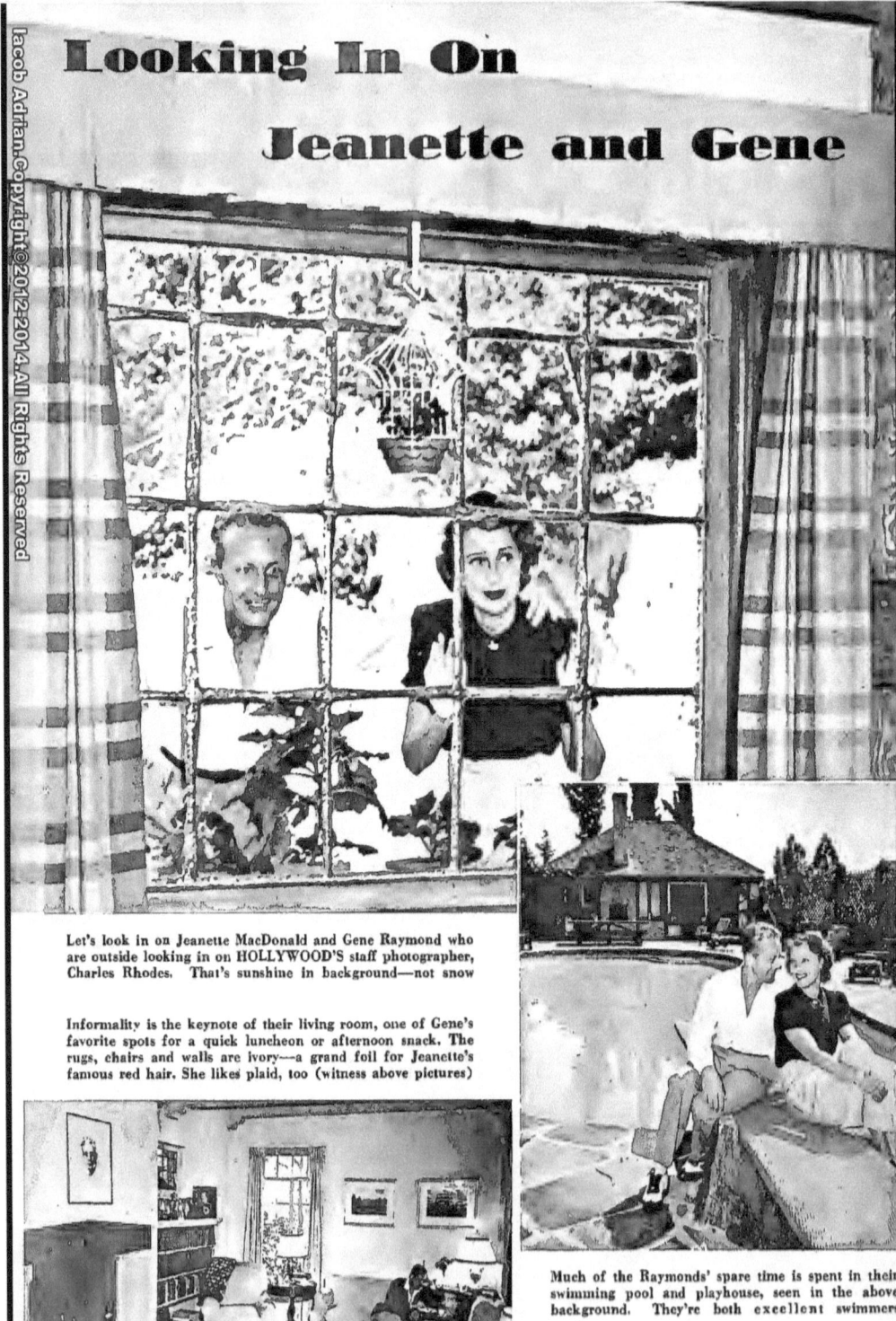

Let's look in on Jeanette MacDonald and Gene Raymond who are outside looking in on HOLLYWOOD'S staff photographer, Charles Rhodes. That's sunshine in background—not snow

Informality is the keynote of their living room, one of Gene's favorite spots for a quick luncheon or afternoon snack. The rugs, chairs and walls are ivory—a grand foil for Jeanette's famous red hair. She likes plaid, too (witness above pictures)

Much of the Raymonds' spare time is spent in their swimming pool and playhouse, seen in the above background. They're both excellent swimmers

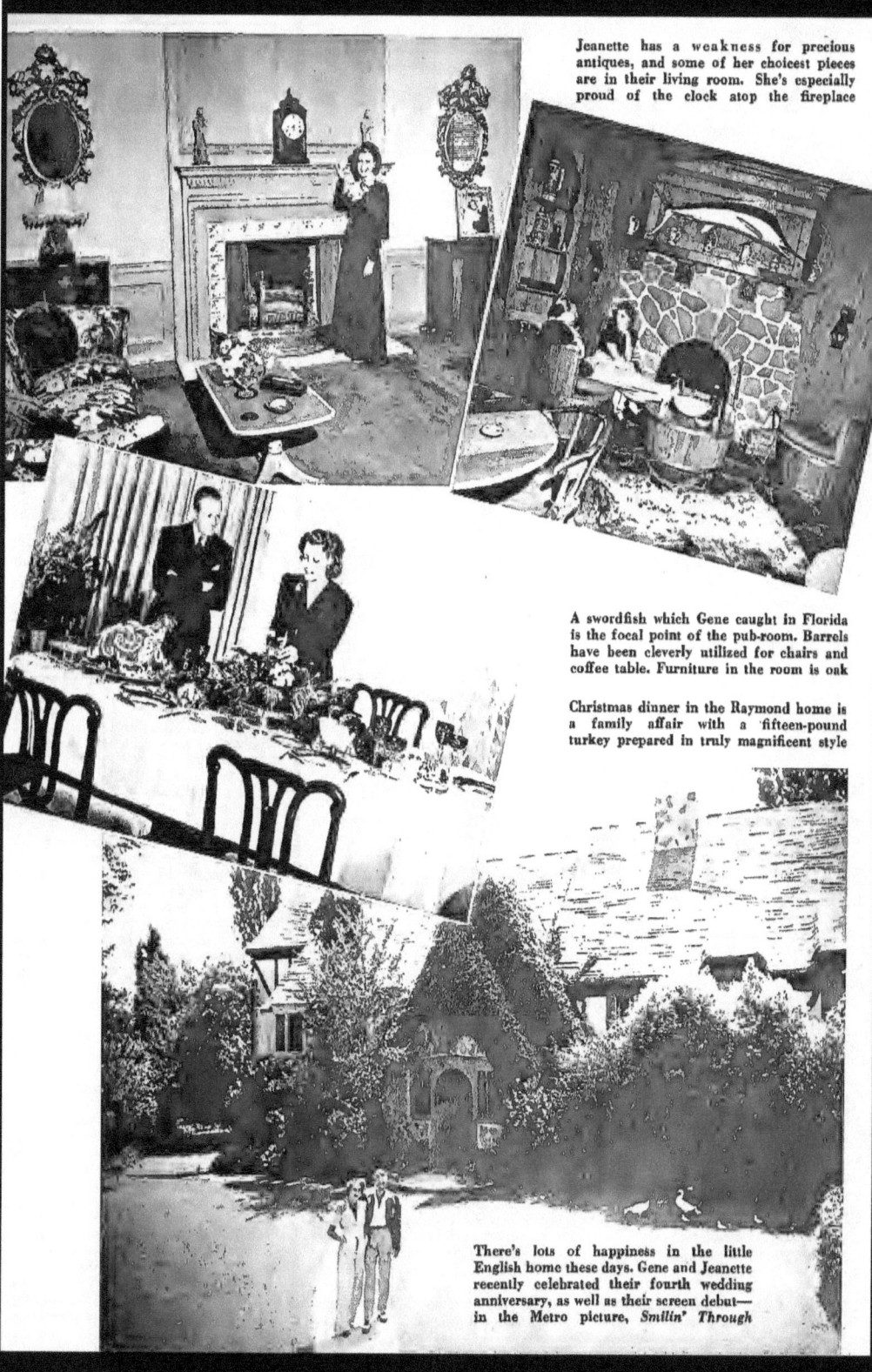

Jeanette has a weakness for precious antiques, and some of her choicest pieces are in their living room. She's especially proud of the clock atop the fireplace

A swordfish which Gene caught in Florida is the focal point of the pub-room. Barrels have been cleverly utilized for chairs and coffee table. Furniture in the room is oak

Christmas dinner in the Raymond home is a family affair with a fifteen-pound turkey prepared in truly magnificent style

There's lots of happiness in the little English home these days. Gene and Jeanette recently celebrated their fourth wedding anniversary, as well as their screen debut— in the Metro picture, *Smilin' Through*

"No, No, Jeanette!"

By MARION COOPER

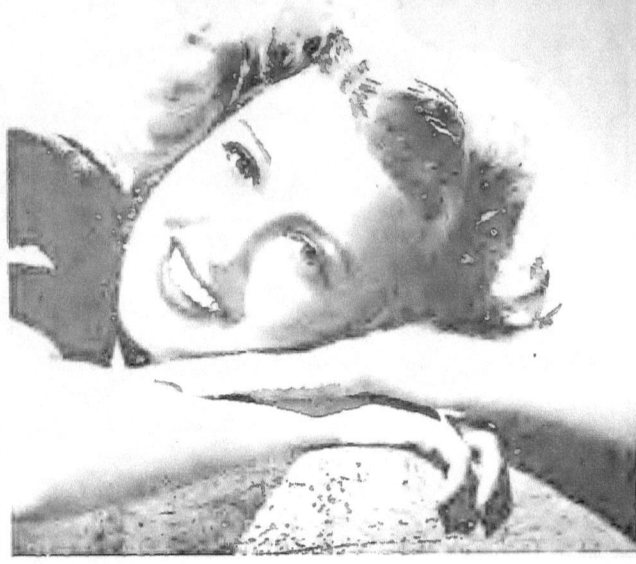

Contrary to popular belief, a singer's life is not an easy one. Jeanette MacDonald almost always has to forego the things she likes, to keep her voice in top form. Jeanette is co-starred again with Nelson Eddy in *I Married an Angel*

Florence was very nervous. It was bad enough to be young and shy, but to be young and shy and about to meet your new boss for the first time was the very worst that could happen to a wardrobe girl. Especially when your new boss was not only a famous movie star but a famous singer as well. Weren't famous singers supposed to be terribly temperamental and accustomed to getting their own way about everything? They didn't know what "no" meant—and they didn't have to learn. Florence was so nervous that she doused herself generously with perfume, subscribing to the general feminine belief that nothing very terrible can happen to you if you smell nice.

Fortified, Florence went in to meet Jeanette MacDonald on the first day's shooting of *I Married an Angel*. Miss MacDonald sniffed the air and immediately asked: "What is that perfume you're using?" Florence beamed, thinking how kind it was of her to notice. "Sandalwood," she told her. Jeanette surprised her by saying, "Well, if you'll promise not to use any during this production, I promise to buy you a big bottle of it as soon as the picture is over."

Florence looked baffled, until Miss MacDonald explained further: "You see, I'm allergic to perfume. It makes me sneeze."

Florence was more surprised than ever. She thought: "Well, here's one singer at least who doesn't get everything her own way. She can't even use perfume!"

"Florence didn't know the half of it," Jeanette said, laughing as she told me about that meeting. "The fact is that any singer who wants to retain a top position, has to forego nearly everything she likes. Take me, for instance," she said, sighing. "Practically every time I want to do something, a little warning sign flashes on and off in my mind, like a neon. 'No, no, Jeanette' it says, 'not good for the stomach or voice.'

"I mustn't eat ice cream or drink milk, they form a coating on the throat. I mustn't eat beans, they give me indigestion. I mustn't eat anything heavy or rich. No, not if I want to go on singing," she said. Suddenly she laughed. "And oh my, the remedies I've tried, the punishment I've taken for Art's sake! Like that time in Springfield, Massachusetts."

That was during a recent concert tour. The nervous strain of traveling, combined with a busy schedule, had conspired to upset her stomach. She was due to sing that evening, and she was desperate. She couldn't sing when indigestion was making her miserable. Suddenly she recalled a conversation she had in Hollywood with Miliza Korjus, a singer too, had the same problems to cope with as Jeanette.

"I used to suffer too," Miliza had said, "it was agony. But no longer," she smiled mysteriously.

"Why no longer?" Jeanette had asked eagerly. "Did you find a cure?"

Miliza had smiled happily. "I have found something that can't miss. Just before a concert I mix raw ground steak with a raw egg, sprinkle it with salt and pepper—and there I am. No discomfort, no indigestion, it's wonderful!"

So in her hotel in Springfield with her stomach doing nip-ups and the time for her concert drawing near, Jeanette remembered Miliza's advice. She lost no time in phoning for the necessary ingredients.

A very puzzled waiter brought them up. He also brought a bottle of Worcestershire sauce, believing apparently that it would make the concoction more palatable.

Jeanette believed so too, after one look at the raw meat and eggs, and added a generous portion of the sauce. Then she forced herself to eat the mixture. It nearly gagged her, but she went through with it, and waited hopefully for results.

They came almost immediately, in the form of the worst attack of indigestion she had ever suffered. What had been Korjus' meat was definitely MacDonald's poison!

"But with a singer," Jeanette continued, "it isn't only what she must and must not eat, but when she must eat it. It's definitely 'no' to the conventional dinner hour, for instance. A singer must eat several hours before she is to sing, in order to give the food time to digest. For that reason, I can't even accept dinner invitations when I'm on a concert tour. Anyway," she smiled, "think how embarrassing it would be to have to refuse practically every dish that was set before me, because it might affect my work!"

It's "no, no" to dancing too, because too much of it dries the throat.

Night clubs are also out, because of the smoky atmosphere.

Drinking is another taboo. "Even if I wanted to, I couldn't," Jeanette confessed. "Every time someone offers me a cocktail, that little 'no, no,' sign pops up."

Only once that she can remember, did this taboo prove embarrassing.

It was after she and Gene Raymond returned from their honeymoon. A friend gave a big party for them. As a crowning touch, two loving cups were passed around, while the guests sang: "Drink it up, drink it down." One cup contained champagne for the ladies, the other vodka for the men. Everyone drank to the happiness of the bride and groom, and then came Jeanette's and Gene's turn.

Jeanette hesitated, that little warning sign flushing on and off in her mind. She hated to spoil the fun by being a poor sport, especially since the drinking was meant as a tribute.

No one noticed her discomfort except Gene, who realized what was bothering her. He whispered in her ear: "Join the singing." She did, and immediately every eye was on her face. Gene drank her portion, the cup was passed on, and everyone was too busy listening to Jeanette to notice. A bad moment was passed, but Gene paid for his gallantry the next morning. Champagne and vodka don't mix!

It's "no, no" to strenuous games like tennis, too, because excitement is bad for a singer's voice. It "roughs it up," Jeanette says. ∎

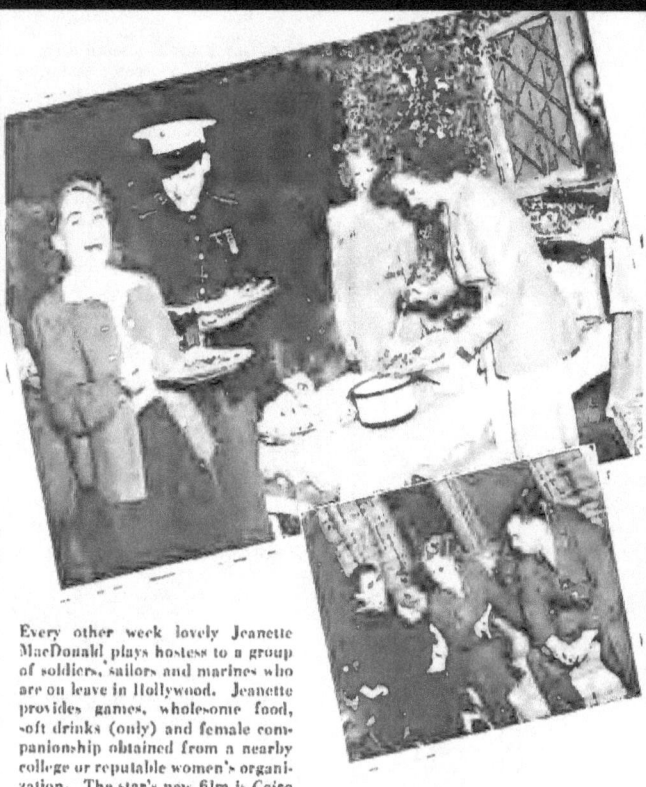

Every other week lovely Jeanette MacDonald plays hostess to a group of soldiers, sailors and marines who are on leave in Hollywood. Jeanette provides games, wholesome food, soft drinks (only) and female companionship obtained from a nearby college or reputable women's organization. The star's new film is *Cairo*

Jeanette MacDonald's
Service Parties

By BETTY CROCKER

For almost a year now, Jeanette MacDonald has been giving a semi-monthly party for the Army, Navy and Marine service men at her Bel Air home. The parties are called "Date-Leaves" and this is how they are planned.

Jeanette tells us the guest list is drawn up every two weeks by the United Service Organization, from among the uniformed young men who are on leave and desire a date.

Then Jeanette receives a list of girls from the Dean of Women at one of the colleges. Both groups are picked up by the Raymond station wagon and arrive before lunch, to be greeted by Jeanette. There are games to play—tennis, ping-pong, or a swim in the pool. After the informal lunch the couples usually dance, or have a song fest, whatever the guests wish. Quite often a jitterbug contest pops up, and Jeanette swings it with the best of them. Finally, well fed and happy, the group is returned.

If you're in a position to help the USO by entertaining a few of our fine young lads in uniform, then you'll want some of Jeanette MacDonald's suggestions.

"I hope lots of people will have 'Date-Leave' parties," Jeanette said, "and give our boys wholesome home food and entertainment.

"My mother has given many such parties, inviting two boys and two girls for an afternoon of badminton or hilarious games of croquet, and a good family dinner. It means so much to the boys so far from home."

Here is a typical "Date-Leaves" menu:

Grilled ground sirloin with special sauce or
Barbecued ham or
Barbecued chicken
Potato salad
Baked beans a la MacRaymond
Hot biscuits—sweet cinnamon rolls

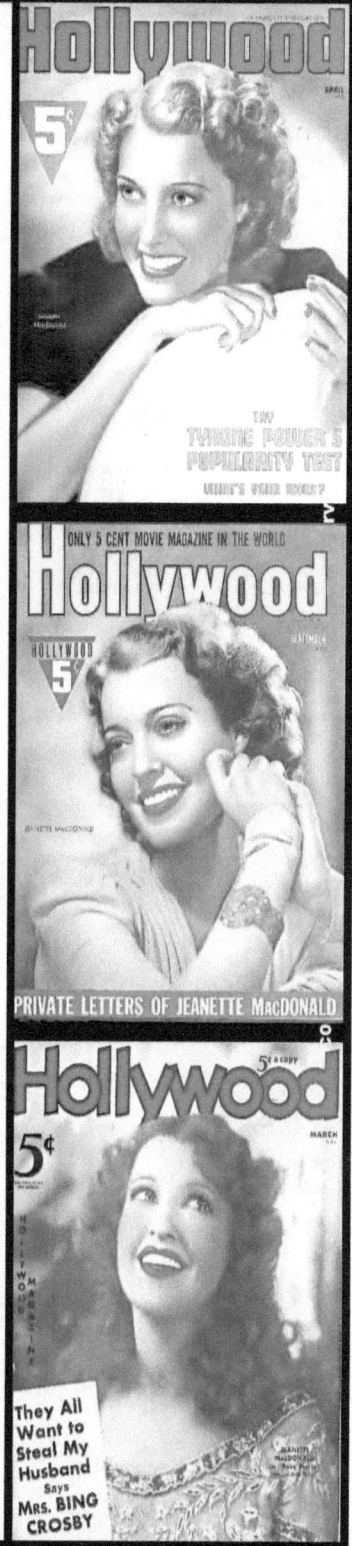

All green combination salad with diced cheese, tomatoes and clear French dressing

Home-made ice cream and chocolate cake

Sirloin is ground with dicings of onion. Add salt and pepper to taste. Special sauce as follows:

One part roquefort cheese, two teaspoons Lee and Perrins sauce, adding enough cream to rub cheese into creamy consistency. Brush paste lightly over each side of steak patty and grill to preferred "doneness."

CHEESE BISCUITS

Add ½ cup grated yellow cheese to 2 cups of prepared biscuit mix. Then add liquid as directed on the package.

CHEESE BISCUIT SANDWICH

Roll out dough for biscuits thinner than usual. Sprinkle grated cheese over half the dough, fold the other half over to cover the cheese and cut out the biscuits. The result will be little biscuit sandwiches with cheese between—almost like toasted cheese sandwiches.

ALL GREEN SALAD

Lettuce, tomatoes, green pepper, celery, green onions, radishes, cucumber, cabbage and ground parsley. Cut into small pieces. Use vinegar and oil dressing.

HOW TO ARRANGE "DATE-LEAVES"

As originated by Jeanette MacDonald and Gene Raymond

Call your local USO headquarters. Tell them how many boys you want to entertain on "Date-Leaves," what day, what time you will call for them and what time you will return them to USO headquarters.

Call the Dean of Women of your local college, or the head of any reputable organization of young women and tell her how many girls you wish to invite. Tell her who you are, what day you are giving a "Date-Leaves."

If your "Date-Leaves" starts just before noon and lasts all day, have sandwiches, cookies, plenty of milk (how they drink that!) on a table where everyone can serve themselves. Mid-afternoon dinner at 3:30. Good-byes are said at 6:00 P.M. The boys are returned to USO headquarters by 6:30. The girls usually provide their own transportation.

The USO approves the fact that only soft drinks are served on "Date-Leaves."

For Recipes and Menus, just address a letter or postcard to Betty Crocker, HOLLYWOOD, 1501 Broadway, New York, and mention "Date-Leaves."

BAKED BEANS A LA MacRAYMOND

Pour layer of freshly cooked beans in a deep old-fashioned bean crock. Over layer of beans place sliced tomatoes or chili sauce. Season with salt and pepper and sprinkle brown sugar over the top. Over this, place sliced bacon or pork chops. Cover casserole and bake in moderately heated oven one and one-half hours—then remove cover and bake fifteen or twenty minutes, allowing chops or bacon to brown.

SAUCY SUSANS

Use tomato juice for liquid in biscuit recipe. Roll dough thin. Cut, and place a round of yellow cheese between each 2 biscuits. Bake close together. These pretty pink biscuits with cheese in them make delicious and unusual salad accompaniments.

HONEY-DATE BISCUITS

Combine 2 cups of prepared biscuit mix with ¾ cup milk as directed on the package and roll out as for biscuit dough. Cream together ¼ cup honey and ¼ cup softened butter. Combine with ¼ cup cut-up dates and ¼ cup pecans, lightly toasted and chopped. Spread this mixture over the biscuit dough. Roll up as for a jelly roll and cut into ¾-inch slices. Place cut side down on a well-greased pan and bake 25 minutes in a moderately hot oven, 400°. This makes 24 small biscuits.

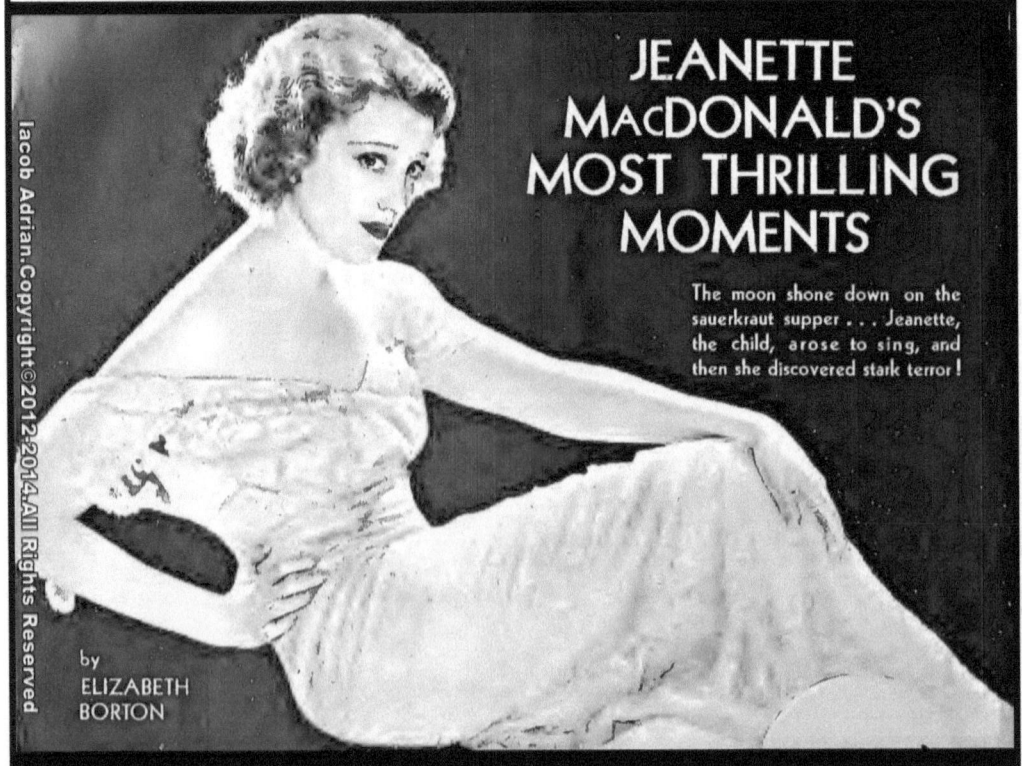

JEANETTE MacDONALD'S MOST THRILLING MOMENTS

The moon shone down on the sauerkraut supper . . . Jeanette, the child, arose to sing, and then she discovered stark terror!

by
ELIZABETH BORTON

Bibliographic sources :

Hollywood (1934-1943)
Publisher: Hollywood Magazine, inc. ; Fawcett Publications, inc.

The New Movie Magazine (1929-1935)
Publisher: Tower Magazines, inc.

This documentary study use,
combined in various proportions,
elements from the following categories,
forms and subsets :
- fair use
- documentary
- documentary photography
- feature
- journalism
- arts journalism
- visual journalism
- photojournalism
- celebrity photography
in order to :
- employ material as the object of cultural critique ,
- quote to illustrate an argument or point ,
- use material in historical sequence,
providing independent opinion,
using photos, press articles, advertisements,
opinions of fans etc. ...